For Jenifer,
You make me a better man.

And for My Children,
I hope and pray that you get this stuff right.

Contents

"Caught between a world that says 'Do it!' and a church that says 'Don't do it!' without explaining why, our kids are floundering. They need more than just the purity talk. They need parents who will step up to the plate. *The Talk(s)* gives you just the blueprint you need to start a lifelong conversation with your kids about intimacy, relationships, and even great sex!"

Sheila Wray Gregoire,
Author of *The Good Girl's Guide to Great Sex*

"As a parent you love your kids. You want to raise them to pursue Godliness, excel in academics and be well rounded in character. Likely you have a plan and coaches, teachers and pastors on your team to help you prepare to launch them! But what is your plan for their moral purity? The book you are holding is your roadmap to doing the heart check God is calling you to do as a parent. It will help you to step up and into the awkward talks of helping your kids guard their hearts and have a plan to confidently face the culture. Read it, pray over the insights you learn, and step boldly into helping your kids win the battle of moral purity!"

Dr. Gary Rosberg
Author of *Guard your Heart*
Speaker, Radio Broadcaster, and Marriage Coach
Americas Family Coaches

"Do you want your children to avoid the sexual and relationship mistakes you made when you were young? It won't happen by accident. It won't happen with wishful thinking. You need a plan! Barrett Johnson's *The Talk(s)* will help you engage your children with loving, practical, and Biblical conversations, not just to guide them away from the disastrous consequences of sexual sin and secrets, but to help prepare them NOW for a joyous and godly future marriage and family of their own."

Dr. Rob Rienow,
Founder of Visionary Family Ministries
Author of *Visionary Parenting*

"With the tidal wave of secular mainstream culture constantly pressing in on our teens and pre-teens, *The Talk(s)* equips parents with the tools they need to fight this battle, and win. Barrett (and Jenifer) Johnson boldly and confidently address the conversations parents need to have with their children, sooner rather than later. I recommend it highly."

Frank Reed
Host, 94.9 KLTY Family-Friendly Morning Show
Dallas/Ft. Worth, Texas

THE TALKS

A parent's guide to critical conversations about sex, dating and other unmentionables.

BARRETT JOHNSON

INFO FOR FAMILIES
resources

Part Three: Becoming the Parent Your Kids Desperately Need

Read This First!

Seriously, Don't Skip Over It.

Let me start this thing off with a potentially awkward statement:

"I want my kids to experience great sex."

God made them as sexual beings with the unique capability to connect powerfully and beautifully with another person. Unfortunately, we live in a world where many people get sex wrong. What God designed to be wonderful becomes the source of some of their greatest pain in life.

I desperately want my kids to get it right.

God has used three key seasons of my life to move me to a sense of urgency regarding this issue: fifteen years of ministering to teenagers, a decade of working with young married adults, and most powerfully, being in the trenches of parenting my own five children.

When I was a youth minister in my 20's, I encouraged kids to strive for sexual purity for the typical reasons: evading disease, avoiding an unwanted pregnancy, and embracing the noble desire to save themselves sexually for marriage. These are all still important reasons, but there are bigger issues at stake. In recent days, I have encountered a body of research that clearly suggests that young people who have their first sexual encounter in their teen years have double the risk of divorce once they are married. More than just risking an STD, sexually active teens are significantly crippling their ability to be successful in a long-term marriage. That is huge.

Jump ahead ten years and I can see that this research is true. As I have worked with young married couples for the past decade in a large evangelical church, I have come to realize that much of the brokenness in the area of married sexuality got started in them long before they walked the aisle. For many, the experiences and mistakes of the teen years made for a dramatically compromised foundation on which to build a healthy marriage and sex life. The result is often pain and regret. I feel for these couples and wish that I could easily fix the hurt from their past.

Beyond the masses of people in the church who I see greatly affected by sexual and relational brokenness, I have particular concern for my own children. My wife Jenifer and I are beginning to launch the five kids we have been raising for the past twenty years. We are daily in the midst of helping our four adolescents have healthy opposite-sex relationships, manage hormonal changes, and maintain a vibrant faith, all within the context of a decaying moral landscape. It is a daunting task and we often feel overwhelmed.

But we are seeing fruit from our labors.

Our oldest daughter got married a little over a year ago. Lindsey and her young husband have allowed God to weave a beautiful tale of purity, devotion, and intentionality through their love story. They guarded their hearts and saved themselves physically (and emotionally) for each other. There is a strength and joy in their young marriage that I rarely see in couples who marry at 30. Many of the people who have watched Lindsey and Christian's story unfold over the past four years have asked Jenifer and me what we did as parents to help them to get there.

While we give every bit of credit to God for what He has done, in many ways, this book is a summary of how we have equipped our own children. From the time they were very young, we have tried to prepare them for what relationships, dating, and even the path toward marriage would look like. As they have gotten older, we have included plenty of discussions about their sexuality. Our desire has been to give them an honest and accurate picture of something God made to be spectacular. Just to be clear, this has not happened because we sat them down for a "talk" when they were young. Instead, it has been the result of a long series of talks. In fact, it has been our goal to keep conversations about sex and relationships very normal and comfortable in our home.

Because we have been deliberately walking through these things with our kids for the past fifteen years or so, we have gained a measure of experience. With kids ranging in ages from 6 to 21, I assure you that we have "been there and done that." This book is, in many ways, a guide to what we have learned along the way.

This book is also a call to action.

While parents cannot eradicate sin and its effects from our children's lives, we also shouldn't passively facilitate its power. Since people start developing their perspective of their sexuality (and its place in their lives) when they are quite young, I passionately believe that parents must step up and do all they can now to help their kids to have a healthy sexuality later. Parents of teenagers should already feel the burden of this at some level, but parents of elementary-aged children should take note as well. Thankfully, parents of young kids have the greatest chance to help their kids to get this right long before they have the chance to get it wrong.

We have had the opportunity to speak on this subject in a number of contexts through the local church. When we teach parents to start talking about sex and dating earlier and in more detail than they might have planned, the reactions we get are all over the map.

Some parents who are also burdened by the direction our culture is headed have expressed appreciation that someone is finally talking openly about how to think Biblically about these issues.

A few others have told us that we are just plain nuts. Backwards. Old-fashioned. They say we are suggesting an unrealistic standard in today's culture. I get that. The principles and ideas found within this book are pretty counter-cultural. However, the last time I checked, just about everything Christ calls his followers to do is counter-cultural. I don't think how we approach sexuality and relationships are exempt from that.

Perhaps the most encouraging response has been from parents who have both teenagers and younger elementary kids in their homes. They have struggled through these issues with their older teens and are now committed to being more proactive with their younger children.

However, I think the masses of people we have taught have been more stunned than anything. We have seen deer-in-the-headlights looks from many. We have invited them to consider a perspective that they, up to now, may have never heard before. For them, our prayer is that they would continue to talk about it, study the issues, and ask God for His insights into their kids and their unique situations. It has been a tremendous joy to hear the stories of parents becoming more intentional and of the difference it is making in their families.

This is a difficult subject with few easy answers. There are some good principles that should guide us, but there are few hard and fast rules that are applicable to every family. These pages do not contain what many books offer, like the "seven steps to guarantee that your kids stay pure." In fact, I have specifically organized this book as a collection of essays that I pray will resonate with different people in different ways. Hopefully, God will speak those exact things that each parent needs to hear. In addition, Jenifer will chime in occasionally with her perspective on things. She's both brilliant and practical.

One final word: I would be irresponsible if I did not clarify something from the very beginning. This book is based upon Christian principles and values. It advocates a view that assumes that God has called people to save sex for monogamous marriage: one partner for life. If you believe that teenagers are inevitably going to have sex and that there isn't anything that anyone can do about it, you're probably not going to like what I have written here. You might even get mad. (This book doesn't talk about the world's version of safe sex. If you embrace that perspective exclusively, then I suggest you find a different book...and that you buy your kids some condoms and teach them how to use them.) But if you think it is possible for your kids to embrace a belief system that will enable them to control their desires for meaningful reasons, then read on.

Our ultimate goal in dealing with these issues has not been to convince anybody that our perspective is right and theirs is wrong. We simply want to encourage parents to carefully consider the long-term effects of how they are leading and protecting their kids in regards to their sexual and relational well-being. Moreover, we want them to make sure that God is involved in their choices. He wants us to look to Him for direction and help as we address these things with our kids. The good news is that He is always with us!

Whether your kids are 6 or 16, the clock is ticking. May we join God in helping our kids to discover—in the right way and in the right time—just how unbelievably amazing He made relationships, sex and marriage to be.

- Barrett Johnson

Part One:
You Have Put This Off
Long Enough

one

Time Travel

*Used DeLoreans and Flux Capacitors are hard to
come by...and that's a problem.*

It happened again.

With sincere angst in their voice, another good parent of another good teenager told me of their dilemma. The parent is bewildered as to what to do about their teen's "opposite-sex" issues. Sadly, I keep hearing the same stories:

One dad is concerned that the cute "boy crazy" behavior his daughter exhibited when she was ten has evolved into something entirely different at 15. She seems obsessed with making sure that she always has a boyfriend. Then she gets depressed when she doesn't have one.

As her teenagers have begun dating, a mom is insistent upon putting some guidelines in place for whom they should date and what they should be allowed to do. Her husband, on the other hand, feels that their kids can figure things out on their own. He figures that they will learn best if they learn the hard way.

A dad worries that his Christian daughter's relationship with her non-Christian boyfriend has gotten way too serious. What started out as a friendship has evolved into something way more significant.

He is beginning to notice how their differences are affecting his daughter's behavior and priorities. Unfortunately, the daughter doesn't see a problem.

But the stories get more complicated. Beyond the typical dating struggles that young people have had to work through for generations, many of the issues today have a sexual dimension.

A mom and a dad are concerned about the pornographic websites that they have discovered in their son's computer history. They aren't sure if this is normal teen behavior that should be left alone or if they should confront him about it.

A dad shares with frustration that his 14-year-old son is overwhelmed by the sexually aggressive nature of the girls at his middle school. Their never-ending texts and flirtations are building his ego, but the drama of it all is distracting him from just about everything else in life. The dad is worried that the temptation of it all will be too much for his son to handle.

A mom is troubled that her 17-year-old daughter has been dating the same boy for more than a year. She has reasons to believe that they have become sexually intimate, but she is not sure how to broach the subject with her; or with him.

I feel for these parents. They want to do all they can to coach their teenagers through some very emotionally taxing and extremely hormonally charged seasons of life. As I work with families in the local church, I encounter lots of them. When they come to me for help, I do my best to provide them with Biblical wisdom and practical steps to take.

However, in moments like these, I can't tell them what I REALLY want to tell them. Because what I really want to tell them is this:

You need to get your hands on a time machine. That's right. You heard me: a time machine. Just like Marty McFly used in Back to the Future. *Used DeLoreans are pretty cheap these days and surely you can find directions for making a flux capacitor online somewhere. Once you finish building it, use your time machine to go back to a time when your kids were very young, very innocent, and very open to your parental perspective and influence.*

Once you have successfully removed yourself and your child from the tumultuous stage of life they are currently in and into a climate when they are a blank canvas regarding the opposite-sex, you can start preparing them for what lies ahead. You can deal with the issues that you already know they are going to face. Best of all, you can do it before they are a raging cauldron of hormones and all caught up in the drama usually associated with boyfriend/girlfriend relationships.

But I can't give that advice, because the last time I checked, time machines aren't readily available to the public. (Though I think they can still be found in Hollywood.)

What is a Parent to Do?

For those currently in the middle of challenging struggles like the ones mentioned above, know that there is a God who wants to walk through these things with us. He offers hope to even the most hopeless of situations. He wants us to trust in His ways for coaching our kids to healthy relationships with the opposite-sex today and, if they choose to marry, to a long and satisfying marriage in their future. Much of this book is about helping to equip parents for that very purpose.

Since an ounce of prevention is worth a pound of cure, we must begin talking about these things with our kids.

The million-dollar question is "When?" As parents wanting to prepare our kids well, when do we explain where babies come from? When do we discuss opposite-sex attraction? When do we start laying some ground-rules for dating and modesty and what to look for in a mate? When do we start talking to our kids about pornography and even masturbation?

Every child is different and every family's situation is unique, but I would suggest that, given the sexually charged culture our kids are growing up in, if the big question is "When?" then there is a common answer for every parent.

The answer is, "Sooner than you think." Take whatever age you think would be best and subtract a few years. Maybe three or four.

Parents need to start training and preparing their kids for this stuff sooner than we think, because our kids will be encountering these issues far sooner than we could ever imagine. If we want them to have a Biblical (and even a holy) perspective of their sexuality, then we must begin to paint that picture to them before the world messes it up.

I used to say that parents need to "get these issues on the table," but the reality is that they are already on the table. Our kids are being exposed to a constant stream of messages from their friends and the media and the world about relationships and sex. Most of these messages are far from the truth. Okay, let me be blunt: they are outright lies. These lies have the power to create in our kids a worldview that will impact their sexuality and their marriages for the rest of their lives. And these issues are definitely on the table.

Instead of telling parents to "get these issues on the table," what I now direct parents to do is this: "Get these issues on *your* table." Current research, common sense, and the Biblical directive all scream this one truth: parents have significant power and influence over this dimension of their kids' lives. Moms and dads must enter into the discussion early and start defining some truths before the world begins to overwhelm their kids with lies. They must boldly start building a framework of truth and preparing their kids for the challenges that they will inevitably face. They must start talking about sex with their kids.

This is a much better option than what most parents typically do. Most parents neglect any meaningful discussions of relationships and sexuality. They push these topics way off into the future, thus exercising the parental equivalent of coaching on game day. They operate with the false assumption that there will be more time and that these issues can wait until their kids are older. This strategy usually results in parents who are caught off guard once they realize that their kids have grown up far faster than they ever dreamed.

The results are pretty typical:

Parents who are shocked when their little girls transform into beautiful young women practically overnight.

Parents who notice their little boys starting to notice those same young women when baseball was their only vice just yesterday.

Parents scrambling to play catch-up once their teenage kids are in the throes of an emotional relationship with the opposite-sex.

Parents wishing they could jump into their time machine and do more to prepare their kids for what lies ahead.

Again, I am convinced that we must start preparing our kids to navigate relationships and their sexuality far sooner than we want to. An honest look at a few statistical realities of teenagers today should wake us up to the urgency of these issues.

- 48% of high school students in America have had sexual intercourse.[1]
- By the time they turn 19, 70% of teens have had oral sex.[2] Most do not consider oral sex to count as "real sex."
- Two out of five girls aged 14-19 have a sexually transmitted disease.[3]
- Only about one third of teenagers agree with the statement: "A young couple should not live together unless they are married."[4]
- The average age of first–time exposure to pornography is 11 years old.[5]
- Of an online support group of porn addicts, more than half said that they got addicted between the ages of 12 and 14.[6]
- 83% of teens say that moral truth depends on the situation.[7]

That last statistic is the most troubling. More and more young people are navigating their circumstances without any clear moral compass of truth. Our children desperately need guidance and they need their parents to help provide it.

The Vital Role of Mom and Dad

In recent days there has been a renewed commitment among many parents to the charge given in Deuteronomy 6:6-7. As Moses gives an extensive overview of the ways and laws of God, he reminds us of the essential role of parents in passing on a legacy of faith to the next generation. He puts it this way:

"These commandments that I give you today are to be on your hearts. Impress them on your children. Talk about them when you sit at home and when you walk along the road, when you lie down and when you get up."

While the content of this training certainly includes essentials like the Ten Commandments and the foundational message of the gospel, it must also include, among other things, teaching our children about God's design for their sexuality. Because it is and will always be a critical part of who they are, they must be taught and prepared for what lies ahead. And it is parents who must do the teaching.

This will obviously include the birds and bees conversation (known by most parents as "the talk"), but it cannot stop there. Our kids desperately need someone to tell them about how the opposite-sex thinks. They need someone to coach them through some physical changes and feelings that they do not fully understand. They need someone to answer the questions they have (but that they might never verbalize). They need someone to protect them from some of the relationships and circumstances that the enemy might use to bring them great harm. By necessity, this will include a long series of talks, not just the one "talk" that most parents focus on. God has given this job to parents. Sadly, most parents have severely neglected it.

There has been a great deal of research in recent days on the sexual perspectives of teenagers. We can learn a lot about their opinions and their behaviors and the impact these things have on their development. These findings are certainly valuable as they paint a vivid picture of the world in which our kids are living.

However, I have discovered a much more reliable source of information on the effects that these early emotional relationships and sexual experiences are having on our young people. It is the honest and raw stories that are shared with Jenifer and me in our ministry to newlywed couples. What should be the most rewarding, satisfying and carefree season of their adult lives is often tainted with a sense of regret.

These young adults are just a few years removed from their intensely emotional teen years. Their memories and experiences are fresh in their minds, but they bring a perspective and a clarity that often comes in the early days of marriage. They certainly don't have it all figured out yet, but they are far enough along to be able to both reflect on their younger years and to clearly articulate their disappointment.

What we commonly hear from these young married couples is their regret that they failed to save themselves sexually for their husbands or wives. On an emotional level, they wish that they had not given their heart away to so many people. The guys are surprised that their struggles with lust and pornography do not miraculously disappear once they are married. The girls, reflecting on the times that they felt taken advantage of by many of the boys they dated, express that they felt completely unprotected by their parents.

> *Jenifer's Perspective:*
> *"I'm stunned by how often I hear young women tell*
> *me that they wish their dads would have guarded*
> *them better during their dating years."*

The most common thing we hear from these sharp, young couples is that they wish their parents had done more to guard their hearts. They wish that their parents had done more to keep them from making the stupid mistakes that they now regret. As they share their stories and we hear their hearts, I often wish we could bottle up their words, put them in our time machine, and share their desperate longings with their younger selves. And with their parents.

Sadly, there is no time machine. These young adults must count on the grace of God to heal their hurts and restore the broken places of their sexuality. Be assured that He can. There may be some struggle along the way, but our God is still in the business of making broken things whole again. For some people, it may be a restoration process they work through all their lives, but our God is capable.

Wouldn't it be better, though, if the Spirit of God could lead and empower parents to address these things with their children and teenagers before things get too broken? Instead of parents wishing with regret for a time machine that will never come, wouldn't it be better if parents looked to God to give them power and direction for how to prepare and protect their kids before they experience the devastating pain of sexual sin?

From all that we have seen, we know that it would be much better.

For that to happen, each of us must be willing to get these issues on the table. On *our* tables. We are going to have to start talking about them with our kids and we must do it sooner than we think. There must be a sense of urgency that only comes when we take an honest look at the culture in which our kids are being raised. We must ultimately believe with passion and conviction that the early sexualization of our kids is a bad thing.

Sadly, I do not think we are convinced. We don't think it is that big of a deal. Be assured...

It is.

two

High Stakes

*Premarital sex is like a time bomb with a slow fuse
that won't blow up until marriage.*

When I was in college, I took a basic anthropology course as part of the science requirement for my liberal arts degree. I confess that it was attractive to me because it was a science credit that didn't involve memorizing a lot of scientific Latin terms or doing any math. Please don't judge; I was only 19.

During that one semester, I learned that anthropologists study different cultures to determine how and why people behave the way they do. They look at physical traits, traditions, rituals, and all the other things that define a people group. While trying to avoid being ethnocentric, they often try to identify what things work in a particular culture for the greater good of the people.

A few years ago, I started pondering this question: What would an unbiased anthropologist from another culture see if he were to carefully study the relationship, dating and sexual norms of young people in our western culture? If he were to write a report of his findings, what would he see as typical and normal behavior? While there would be slight variations in different countries, his observations and report would probably look something like this:

Elementary School

Boy/girl interaction is limited as boys tend to congregate with boys and girls with girls. There is some interplay between the genders, though it has very little to do with sexual interest. Of course there are some exceptions: talk of "Ethan likes Ashley" can be heard on the playground, but it is more of an awkward embarrassment than based on any real intentional pursuit of a relationship. For the vast majority, elementary-aged girls think that boys are gross and elementary aged boys think girls aren't worth the effort.

Early Middle School

While most 6th grade students don't typically have an interest in the opposite-sex, there are a few "early bloomers" who do, and they often set the pace for the rest of the kids. Put these 11-year-olds in a middle school environment that includes some older 8th graders and this group is ripe for indoctrination into a boyfriend/girlfriend culture. Some 6th graders even begin an early form of dating. Talk of "who is hot" in the class is not uncommon.

Later Middle School

By the 7th and 8th grade years, playful flirtation gives way to the actual pairing of couples. What previous generations referred to as "going steady," most young people today refer to as "going out" (though nobody really goes anywhere). Most of these "relationships" have little substance beyond the kids being able to declare that they are "together," but that doesn't stop them from expressing their affections via text message or on whatever social media site is popular that week. Because girls tend to mature faster than boys at this stage, most girls take the relationships very seriously while their male counterparts don't put much emotional energy into them. This can be explosive when the boy loses interest and the girl is left heartbroken.

Early High School

Interest in boy/girl relationships intensifies at a rapid pace as boys begin to catch up with girls in both emotional and sexual maturity. In a significant way and driven by a variety of hormonal and cultural influences, boys begin to notice girls. Clearly defined relationships develop that tend to be brief but that occasionally have the endurance to last several years. While interaction within a particular relationship at school, work, or church may be extensive, it often doesn't compare to the never-ending connection made possible by cell phones and social media. The tendency to become "obsessed" with the relationship is a real possibility. The music, TV, and movies targeted at adolescents further affirm the normalcy of emotionally and physically significant relationships. Those high school students who have a regular diet of such media tend to develop a perspective that such relationships are both expected and necessary. It is during this age that the emotional connection within boy/girl relationships can become extremely powerful.

Later High School

As young people begin to drive and work (and thus have more disposable income), couples who are "going out" together will actually begin going out together. Freed from the restrictions of parents and the limitations of group activities, these relationships can turn physical very quickly. Depending on the couple, it is not uncommon for them to see intimate kissing, sexual touching, oral sex, and even intercourse as normal, reasonable dimensions of their relationship. Even for those who do not have a boyfriend or girlfriend, the need to be wanted by another can be quite powerful. Particularly for girls, self-worth can be tied up in whether or not anyone is taking an interest in them.

The College Years

Many see this stage as a time when it is desirable to date around and even to experiment sexually. After all, they reason, the confines of mature adulthood are just around the corner so they need to get it out of their systems before they settle down. While there are emotional risks associated with this behavior, this stage of life is seen as one in which a marriage partner is likely to be identified, so "playing the field" is encouraged. Because of an increased sexual drive and a greater capacity for mature relationships, couples tend to become both sexually and emotionally intimate at a much more rapid rate. Unfortunately, these relationships can dissolve just as quickly.

Young Adulthood

Adults in their 20's are typically divided into two groups. One group (made up mostly of men) primarily wants their relationships to be an outlet for fun and for sexual activity. While they may hold jobs and be productive members of society, it doesn't stop them from seeking an extended adolescence free from the responsibilities of adulthood. The other group is made up of young adults who are dating in hopes of finding a mate. They are exploring their options and trying different people out to determine who might be a good fit for them in marriage. While these two groups have different motivations, most will eventually end up married. Both are made up of individuals who will find themselves in various relationships until they find "the one."

Does This Characterize Our Kids?

Take a moment to consider people you know who are currently in each of these life stages. Most would fit rather neatly into these descriptions. Their actual behavior may not be reflected there, but it is likely that they would agree that these activities are normative for their peers and well within the boundaries of acceptable tendencies and practices. Few would be shocked or troubled by what an unbiased anthropologist might conclude about their generation.

What about the parents of these kids? Should the beliefs and practices of their children as described by our fictional anthropologist trouble them at all?

The response of most *Christian* parents to these realities is to assume that, while this dating/relationship pattern might be true for their kids, the parts related to sexual intimacy are not. After all, their children are being raised with a different set of values: Biblical values. Their kids know better and will not put themselves into these types of situations.

Think again.

A recent study conducted by The National Campaign to Prevent Teen and Unplanned Pregnancy determined that 88% of unmarried 18- to 29-year-olds are having sex. When looking at our general population, that number is not surprising. However, when they looked only at *evangelical Christian* young adults, the number dropped to 80%.[1] That's an 8-point improvement by Christians over the general population. Yippee.

Read that again. Eight out of ten young single adults who identify themselves as evangelical Christians are having sex. While I support the abstinence movement, research shows that well-intentioned pledges of purity are not sufficient.

The reason we must look at both the dating habits of our kids AND the sexual habits of our kids is that they are so closely related. Teenagers (particularly those who will become the 80% mentioned above) don't just decide one day that they want to have sex and then go looking for someone to accommodate them. No, most find themselves in an intimate emotional relationship that slowly transitions into a physically intimate one. That reality alone should lead parents to move their teaching away from "don't have sex" and toward "guard your heart." More on that later.

The Consequences We Know

Casual sexual activity is a very big deal, as there are significant consequences to physical intimacy outside of marriage. Nevertheless, I want to suggest that the consequences are bigger and broader than most of us realize. The long-term effects of this sexual activity go well beyond the "usual suspects" that we typically hear about. What are the usual suspects? We know them well:

Premarital sex can lead to an STD.

While Sexually Transmitted Diseases have been around for ages, the AIDS epidemic of the past 25 years has made everyone more aware of the health risks of casual sex. Unfortunately, the global response to this has not been a call to radical purity but to a worldwide indoctrination on the merits of "protected" sex. So, while STD's are a significant consequence of premarital sex, if a condom can help us to avoid them, their impact is potentially minimized. (Even though many young people regularly have unprotected sex.)

Premarital sex can lead to an unplanned pregnancy.

The statistics on this issue are absolutely staggering. Thirty percent of unmarried evangelical Christian women between the ages of 18 and 29 have experienced a pregnancy.[2] Though we always want to celebrate life, we can assume that the vast majority of these were unplanned. The impact of pregnancy on a single woman is far-reaching, whether she chooses to keep the baby, to give it up for adoption, or to end its life through abortion.

Premarital sex can leave significant emotional wounds.

The bond that sex creates between two people can leave a vulnerable young person with significant emotional wounds once the relationship dissolves. This is often the source of the "drama" that we see associated with young love. Unfortunately, the emptiness associated with a break-up can often drive a person in pain to seek relief in another relationship. If that isn't available, our culture encourages him or her to bury the hurt deep and move on with head held high. The result is the false assumption that the young person learned some good lessons and matured through the process.

The usual suspects mentioned above are significant, but they are only the tip of the proverbial iceberg. We notice them and are troubled by them, mainly because they are right out in front for all of us to see. We hear about it when a friend of a friend dies of AIDS. We are deeply saddened by it. Unless they quietly get an abortion, we know when a distant family member's daughter gets pregnant. We furrow our brows and reflect on her troubling circumstances. We get to witness first-hand when our teenager has a broken heart. It discourages us, at least until we see her move on.

If we focus on these obvious things and ignore what lies beneath the surface, we might be tempted to believe that, for most of our young people, their early relational (and even sexual) experiences are all a natural, healthy part of growing up. However, something much bigger is at stake.

The Big Consequence: A Premarital Time Bomb

If the greatest impact of premarital sexual activity isn't those usual suspects, then what is it? What, exactly, is the big problem that lies beneath the surface of all of this? What is the big part of the iceberg? Here is what is at stake:

> *Today's premarital sexual activity, fostered mainly by premarital relational intimacy, has significant power to negatively impact a person's future marriage, both sexually and relationally. To put it bluntly, the more our kids play the field, the greater the likelihood that their eventual marriage will end in divorce.*

I often work with married couples in crisis, helping them to sort through their issues. As I talk with them and delve into their history, I can see the far-reaching impact of their premarital relationships. In a word, the more emotional connections an individual had before marriage, the harder it is for them to make a uniquely powerful emotional commitment to their spouse. The more sexually active a person is before marriage, the harder it is for them to have a meaningful sex life in marriage.

What is ultimately at stake for our kids is the very stability of their future marriages. South African pastor P.J. Smyth captures it this way:

> *When I lived in Harare, Zimbabwe, close to our flat was the most enormous hole in the ground about the size of half a football field, and at least 40 meters deep. It was the foundation for a huge skyscraper office building. The bizarre thing was that during the pause in the work between digging*

23

the hole and starting to build, the site was totally unguarded for a few weeks. If I had the desire I could have got down into the bottom of the hole without much difficulty. Why were there no guards? Because there was nothing to protect, of course! But let's imagine that for some reason I wanted to destroy the building. Rather than take a wrecking ball to it once it was up, I would be cunning to sneak down into the unguarded foundation, dig a couple of grave-size holes, lay some explosives that I set on a three year fuse, cover it over, climb out, walk away and relax for three years! And the beauty of it would be that they would probably never suspect that it was me! The foundation of your marriage is your pre-marriage years. If Satan can sneak in and mess you up during those foundational years, then he is well on the way to destroying your marriage in the future. The masterstroke of satanic genius is to make you believe that marriage only begins when you say, "I do."[3]

I recognize the effects of this "pre-marriage time bomb" in the marriages I see struggling today, but I only see the problems being compounded for our children's generation. They are growing up in a culture that is more sexualized, encourages more casual relationships, and is loading them with more emotional baggage than their parents' generation ever experienced.

But just don't listen to me. Research from a variety of sources has shown that the relational and sexual issues of our younger years can significantly affect our adult relationships.

In 2011, the University of Iowa studied the link between teenage sex and divorce rates in women. Published in *The Journal of Marriage and Family*, their research concluded that women who lose their virginity as teens are far more likely to divorce. Of married women who had sex for the first time as teens, 31% were divorced within 5 years. In addition, 47% were divorced within 10 years. In contrast, married women who delayed sex into adulthood had a divorce rate of 15% at 5 years and 27% at 10 years.[4] That's twice the likelihood of divorce at the five-year mark and near double at the ten-year mark.

A study done at Western Washington University showed that when a woman had premarital sex with just one partner before her spouse, she tripled the risk of divorce when compared with those who married as virgins.[5]

A classic study of roughly 10,000 women by The Heritage Foundation in 1995 discovered some very interesting truths related to premarital sexual activity and later marital success/satisfaction. Through a variety of factors, they concluded that "women are best off in life if they are sexually active only within the bounds of marriage. Increases in the number of non-marital sex partners are linked to a very broad array of negative life outcomes." Among their findings was that 80% of women who had no previous sexual partners before their husband were in stable marriages. In contrast, only 44% of women who had just two previous sexual partners before their husband were currently in a stable marriage.[6] Again, that's nearly double the problems in marriage for young women who are sexually active before marriage.

Here's the bottom line of the aforementioned research: *those who guard their sexuality have somewhere between two and three times the likelihood of marital success than those who have, by the world's standards, even just a little sexual experience.* While STD's and teen pregnancy get most of the attention, the potential failure of our kids' future marriages is the broadest and most troubling consequence of premarital sex.

Let me make a very unpopular observation. Early boy/girl relationships, especially those among younger teens, offer very little in terms of an upside. In contrast, the downside is far-reaching. It is like starting the clock on a time bomb that will sit quietly by until our kids enter marriage. We do not know how big the explosion will be, but the chances are that it WILL explode. As parents, we must realize that our kids have no way of understanding these long-term effects. It is up to us to lead and guide them in the way that is best.

In his excellent book *Forbidden Fruit: Sex and Religion in the Lives of American Teenagers,* Mark Regnerus studied the tendency for young people (even Christian young people) to throw themselves into deeply emotional and physical bonds with no awareness of the consequences. He summarizes the typical Christian parent's perspective on these shallow relationships. He says, "Presently, we are threatening to not only accept such half-baked relationships, but even encourage them."[7]

I love how a respected social researcher characterizes the boyfriend/girlfriend relationships that most of our teenagers pursue: he calls them "half-baked." In many ways, he is more clued in than most Christian parents. We think it's wonderful when our kids have a "significant other" because it shows that they are fitting in to the culture nicely. We might even affirm how "cute" it is, unconcerned about how the relationship might evolve into something not so cute. It proves how much we have bought into the world's idea of what is right.

We would do well to remember the words of Romans 12:2: *"Don't be conformed to this world...."* Believers are called to be set apart and different. We should never use the standard of culture as the standard for our lives.

The accepted dating practices of our culture are leading to off-the-chart levels of sexual activity in our kids. We can try to deny this or downplay it, but it remains true. The research screams that this premarital sexual activity can lead to an extremely compromised marriage in the future. The foundation for a successful marriage is established long before a couple gets engaged and heads to the chapel for their wedding. It starts when our kids are still young and under the influence and protection of their parents.

We have a clear responsibility to give our kids a healthy picture of sex and to put parameters on them so that they will not carelessly mishandle this amazing gift. If we can successfully do this, they will have a far better chance of experiencing God's best once they are married. Wise and visionary thinking is required of us if we are to help our kids to recognize the big part of the iceberg.

Perhaps a parable will help us to understand our role.

three

The Playground

*A parable about your vital role in leading
and protecting your kids.*

There once was a gifted architect who dreamed up the most amazing playground imaginable. His creative talent was matched only by his love for children and his commitment to their joy.

He was committed to building a magnificent place just for them: a place filled with slides and swings and all sorts of things to climb and explore. It would be grand in scale: a playground that kids could go to time and time again, having a new experience every time they visited. He spent many years designing and building his playground. His vision was unprecedented. His construction team was talented. His budget was unlimited.

Finally, the playground was opened. What he created was absolutely amazing.

As the first young children rushed through the gates of what everybody agreed was the most extravagant playground they had ever seen, they noticed every detail that the architect had included. They saw numerous places to play "make-believe": a huge ship with masts to climb, an entire village of houses and stores arranged on a main street, and an enormous inter-connected castle structure that could host elaborate "battles" with friends. They were overwhelmed by all the twisting, curving slides that jutted down from just about every elevated spot within the playground. The children were young, but what they saw let them know that this truly was a special place built just for them.

But there was something important about the playground that the children didn't know. The property was situated at the edge of a large community park. While the land was ideal for a playground, the land adjacent to it was not. On one side was a busy parking lot. On the opposite side was a large drainage ditch. Behind it ran a major six-lane highway.

While the playground was designed with the joy of children as its goal, the hazards around it were significant. The architect knew this. So, in addition to building a great playground, he also built a high fence around it to keep the children safe.

This fence was intentionally designed to keep kids in and to keep danger out. His ultimate motivation was to enable the children to have the best time in the safest environment possible. Because he was the father of a 4-year-old himself, he knew that the typical child would enjoy the playground but be completely oblivious to the dangers around it. He knew that most children would do exactly what his daughter would do.

He knew that his little girl would see the playground long before the car stopped in the parking lot. Due to her excitement, she would want to get out of her car seat long before he could reach back to unbuckle her. He would have to firmly instruct her to hold his hand as they walked across the parking lot, as her temptation would be to hit the blacktop and make a break for it. Once inside the playground, she would be fueled by a non-stop flow of adrenaline and joy that would go until he dragged her away (against her will) hours later.

There was one more thing he was confident of: she would be oblivious to the dangers around the playground. She would not notice the drainage ditch. She would not have any concerns about the parking lot. She would not be aware of the thousands of cars speeding by on the adjacent road. She would only notice the playground and the fun to be found there.

It is for this reason that he had to build the fence. For the thousands of families who would visit in the future, the architect was confident that children would enjoy all the playground had to offer, but he was counting on parents to teach their kids to honor the fence.

He had some concerns that older, more inquisitive (or rebellious) children might see the fence as something to explore. They might think that the playground wasn't sufficient for their fun and feel compelled to climb the fence to see what was on the other side. They might even think that the architect built the fence because he was keeping them from something worthwhile. While nothing could be farther from the truth, he knew that children have a tendency to push against their boundaries.

He could not help this. He had done his part as an architect to build something absolutely wonderful AND to put in place some clear protection from the hazards associated with it. Now he was counting on the children's parents to bring their kids to the playground but also to protect them from the dangers that the children were not mature enough to consider themselves.

A Lesson for Parents

Just as we can miss that Jesus' parable of the prodigal son is more about the attitude of the faithful son than it is about the behavior of the rebellious son, we can miss that the parable of the playground is more about parents than it is about children. Before we consider that, let us first make sure we are all clear on some basic truths found in the parable.

First of all, we must be convinced that a loving and wise God created sex with our greatest joy and pleasure in mind. He is the architect of a powerfully beautiful act that his children can explore and enjoy over and over again. This truth is reflected clearly in his Word.

Jesus quoted Genesis 2 when He said, *"For this reason a man will leave his father and mother and be united to his wife, and the two will become one flesh."* (Matthew 19:5) Paul mentions this truth again in two of his epistles. God wants us to know that the unique physical connection that sex affords us is foundational to the marriage relationship.

In a chapter in Proverbs devoted entirely to sex, Solomon gives his son the following directive: *"May your fountain be blessed, and may you rejoice in the wife of your youth."* (Proverbs 5:18) In contrast to the pain and grief associated with casual sex, Solomon reminds us of the joy and celebration associated with marital intimacy.

In fact, he goes into more explicit detail in his Song of Solomon, an entire book of the Bible that is primarily devoted to the joys of sex. Yes, God is far from being puritanical when it comes to our sexuality. Who else but God could have created such a unique expression of love between two individuals?

In addition to the fact that God made sex to be just plain awesome, we must also recognize that God has given his children some very clear and non-negotiable parameters regarding sexual intimacy. These boundaries are like a fence to ensure that we enjoy what He has created without getting hurt. Though our rebellious nature often leads us to question and to push against these parameters, we must remember that God's law is simply His way of reminding us how He designed the world to work. When we submit to Him and His instructions, we are secure.

While not an exhaustive list, these things might be considered to be portions of God's "fence" around the playground of sex:

We must remember that God designed sexual intimacy to be shared within a covenant heterosexual relationship. Paul drove this point home with the Corinthian church when he reminded them that *"each man should have sexual relations with his own wife, and each woman with her own husband."* (1 Corinthians 7:2) While this command includes intercourse, it also implies any other form of sexual intimacy.

Defining "sexual intimacy" is just as difficult as answering the question that every hormonal teen has asked since the time of Noah: "How far is too far?" While there is room for debate, scripture makes clear that we are to *"flee from sexual immorality. All other sins a person commits are outside the body, but whoever sins sexually, sins against their own body."* (I Corinthians 6:18) If this command is a "fence" that God has given us, a person of wisdom does not climb the fence. He avoids it altogether. Radical sexual purity would be a wise goal for all of us.

Another boundary that God gives for our good is the command to *"not be yoked together with unbelievers. For what do righteousness and wickedness have in common?"* (2 Corinthians 6:14) The blunt implication for relationships is that Christ-followers have no business of marrying (or even dating, I would argue) people who don't share their commitment to Christ.

We will further unpack these directives from God in later chapters, but we must be convinced that each of them is given to us for our good.

Which brings us to the crux of the Parable of the Playground: most of our teenage kids are not convinced. The tendencies and behaviors of even many of our "good kids" prove that they are not fully convinced that God's boundaries regarding their sexual beliefs and practices are necessary.

Like the older, more inquisitive children on the playground who question the fence, teenagers are not likely to appreciate the value of the boundaries that God has given. They live in a world that regularly and systematically communicates a worldview of sex that tends to focus on the playground but entirely ignores the fence. Consider how Kenneth Ryan illustrates this in his book *Finding Your Prince in a Sea of Toads:*

> *In a classic ridiculous movie,* Monty Python and the Holy Grail, *there is a scene in which a supposedly horrible beast is guarding a cave. The knights have heard horror stories about its ferocity, having been told, "It has long claws and horrible fangs. It is a hideous monster," so they approach the cave with great fear and caution. But all they see is a little bunny hopping around in front of the cave. "It's just a bunny," the first knight says in a British accent filled with derision. He approaches the cave casually and the bunny leaps to his throat biting and killing the knight. More knights follow and are slaughtered by the fake-looking killer bunny. It is a classic moment in movie comedy. Sex outside of marriage is like the bunny. It looks like a harmless, fuzzy thing that you would*

want to cuddle. It looks warm, friendly, and desirable. People who warn against the dangers of sex while single are usually considered radical nuts, out of step with modern times. The derision is similar to that of the knights just before they were slaughtered. Many people hear the warnings about premarital sex and think they are not susceptible to its powers. You are surrounded by movies, magazines, TV shows, and friends who all deal with dating sex as if it is a harmless little fluff ball, nothing but fun. Any negative consequences are ignored or laughed at. Everyone seems to think sex is "just a little bunny" until it is too late.[1]

Which brings us back to the critical role of parents and a parable created with them in mind. Parents must be willing to prepare their kids for the joys of sex (God's gift) while being very diligent to teach them to respect the parameters (God's law).

Why? Because our kids are not wise enough to do it themselves.

A four-year-old anxious to enjoy the most amazing playground she has ever seen will go full speed ahead, oblivious to any dangers around her. I have seen this in each of my own children.

Likewise, without clear guidance, teenagers will tend to rush into emotional intimacy and sexual activity without much consideration of the long-term impact of what they are doing. Most simply do not have the wisdom to fully understand why God has put the boundaries in place. Even if they are mindful of the boundaries, they are prone to forget them. Put them in a situation where they are emotionally connected to another and their hormones are firing on all cylinders and anything can happen.

So, again, parents must step in to establish, teach, and even enforce the boundaries God has given His children regarding sex. Because we know things that our kids do not know.

We know the emotional pain that comes from connecting sexually with another, only to see the relationship dissolve. If, by God's grace, we have never experienced that ourselves, we have certainly seen it devastate the lives of others.

We know teenagers who have dealt with unplanned pregnancies and have seen the struggles and difficulties they have encountered.

We know families who have been destroyed by the effects of pornography and rampant lust.

We know that, even in a healthy marriage, making sex work right is an ongoing challenge. Baggage from our past only serves to complicate things further.

God has given us sex to enjoy AND clear guidelines to enjoy it. Teaching our kids to honor both of these components is the biggest lesson in the Parable of the Playground. We must teach our kids that sex is a wonderful gift from God that is to be enjoyed. We must also enforce the fence, even if our kids are oblivious to the need for it. Even if our kids don't like the parameters we set, we do this because we love them.

Jenifer's Perspective:
"The best news in the world is that we do not face this task alone. There is a loving God who has given us direction for how we can all experience His very best for our lives. And He is always with us."

Our greatest goal as parents in this area should be to paint a beautiful picture for our kids of what their sex life will be like one day, while striving to minimize the baggage they take into their marriages. While we cannot fully protect them from the corrupt nature of our world's view of sex, we still must make every effort.

Make no mistake: this is a parent's job. It is one that should be done within the home in the context of a loving parent/child relationship. For even the most well-intentioned attempts by others will be insufficient, mainly because they tend to emphasize all the wrong things. Rabbi Shmuley Boteach captures this perfectly:

I recently met an engaging and attractive teenager, carrying around a robot-baby as part of a High School project, which she had to feed and whose diapers she had to change every few hours—all electronically monitored—to show her the utter burden of having a baby and thereby practice safe sex. How absurd that rather than teach teens that sex is electrifying and loving in marriage but boring and degrading when practiced recreationally, we instead teach young people to avoid having sex because children, at any age, are the ultimate nuisance. High schools and colleges might know a lot of about physics and football. But they should leave Sex-Ed to those who believe that love is something intimate and uniquely human rather than a hormonal urge that ought to be indulged in with a condom.[2]

Our kids need someone to tell them that sex is awesome. They need someone who can cast a vision for how great it will be for them to enjoy it within the safe, committed environment of marriage some day. They need someone who will try to protect them from messing it up or doing it for all the wrong reasons.

That job belongs to us. We are their parents.

four

Foolishness

Encouraging your teenager to enter a serious relationship is like giving plutonium to a preschooler.

Being a part of a large church means that my kids are involved in a lot of student ministry activities. They go to youth camps, on mission trips, and participate in lots of small group meetings. It affords them plenty of opportunities to interact with teenagers from a lot of different backgrounds. I have found that I can get a pretty good snapshot of where kids are at when "sharing" is encouraged in these different contexts.

We all know what I'm talking about:

On the first night of Disciple Now: "Share what you are struggling with."

On the last night of a retreat: "Share what God has done in your life."

In the evenings while on a mission trip: "Share what God is teaching you."

While this is often a great chance to hear stories of how God is moving, it can also serve as a startling window into the relational lives of teenagers. It gets particularly interesting when the genders are separated, as the girls' stories and perspectives have a certain raw emotion to them.

What I am most troubled by is how common it is to hear the girls, some as young as 12 or 13, share the trauma and hardships of their current relationships. As they describe what they are going through and what they are feeling, it is apparent (at least to any adults who are listening) that they are in over their heads. One is crying a river of tears over a clueless 14-year-old boy who had no idea that breaking up via text message was not appropriate. Two other girls, who used to be best friends, are not speaking to one another because one of them talked to the other's boyfriend at a party last weekend. On the other side of the circle, a girl is sobbing because she can't believe that the boy she likes chose someone else. Unfortunately, their peers seem to be encouraging the emotion via an endless supply of hugs and tissues. What was intended to be a time of sharing about Christ quickly becomes a support group of girls with boy problems. It's ridiculous, but it's real.

Maybe the culture these kids are living in is expecting them to grow up too fast. Just maybe.

When Love is Awakened Too Soon

Tucked within the pages of Song of Solomon is a wonderful piece of advice that seems custom-made for our teenagers. In this sometimes racy book that shares the intimate words sung between lovers, we read on three different occasions: *"Do not arouse or awaken love until it so desires."* (Song of Solomon 2:7, 3:5, and 8:4)

While Solomon's bride may have simply been telling the "daughters of Jerusalem" to let her man sleep late, I think there is a deeper meaning here. The entire book is devoted to describing the intense love and passion that is being experienced. It is like a wild beast that, once awakened, cannot be tamed. In that context, the lovers are both describing the powerful force that they now know AND they are warning their younger siblings to not go there until they are absolutely ready to handle it. The experience is so powerful, intoxicating, and life-changing, they had better not unleash it until they are ready. Because once it is awakened, it is difficult to turn off.

Regrettably, our culture encourages our teenagers to awaken love as soon as possible; and as often as possible.

From what I have witnessed, the result is that our kids are forced to grapple with the complications and challenges of giving their fully-awakened hearts away, only to see them trampled on by the carelessness and self-centeredness of others. They just don't have the maturity to handle the circumstances that relationships of that nature typically throw at them.

It is like giving plutonium to a preschooler and telling her to go play with it in the backyard. She's just not equipped or ready to handle it with the care that is needed. And while nuclear materials certainly require an intense level of safekeeping, the reality is that the hearts of our children and adolescents are equally as fragile.

From an early age, God stirs in our children an awareness of the opposite-sex. There is an obvious shift that begins to take place in girls and then a bit later in boys. I have witnessed this shift in each of my children. As parents, our role is not to ignore or suppress this God-given awakening, but to help our children to interpret it and to navigate the potential minefield that goes along with it.

> *Jenifer's Perspective:*
> *"Girls, in particular, have a longing to have a best friend.*
> *Because other girls can be so horrible during the teen*
> *years, we shouldn't be surprised when our daughters seek*
> *out meaningful relationships with boys during that*
> *season. Boys are usually a lot easier to deal with."*

I can remember a time when my oldest daughter Lindsey was in the 5th grade. She started acting a bit strange sometimes when we were at church. I couldn't figure it out, but Jenifer began noticing a pattern to her quirky behavior. I was a youth minister so we were always around teenagers. Whenever Lindsey was around a 9th grader named Matt, her weirdness would surface. Sometimes she would giggle. Sometimes she would be shy. Jenifer finally theorized that Lindsey had something of a crush on Matt. When she asked Lindsey about it, she turned red, so we knew we were on to something.

Now Matt was a great guy. He was friendly, handsome, and Christ-like: exactly the kind of guy that we would love for our daughters to marry one day. At that point, it was critical for Jenifer and me to coach a 5th grade Lindsey about what was stirring within her and to help her to realize that she was in no way ready to fan the flames of affection towards Matt. We were intentional to affirm the good things she saw in him and to encourage her to keep looking for the right traits in boys so she would be prepared to give her heart to the right guy down the road sometime.

The message the world is giving our kids is radically different than God's Truth. Everything our kids get from the world says to "follow your heart." They hear that message in their movies, in their music, and in the very ethos of their generation. They have been fed a steady diet of that type of drivel from the Disney princess movies they watched when they were preschoolers to the top-40 music they listen to today. It is what they know by default.

In contrast, Jeremiah 17:9 tells us about the questionable reliability of the heart: *"The heart is deceitful above all things and beyond cure. Who can understand it?"* According to Scripture, following one's heart can be synonymous with following a lie. It cannot be trusted and it is not always reasonable. However, because of their lack of experience and their exposure to the "trust your heart" message, our kids may not know any other way.

Thus, instead of "follow your hearts," we must deliberately train our kids to "guard their hearts." Proverbs 4:23 gives Christ-followers that very command: *"Above all else, guard your heart, for everything you do flows from it."*

A Primer on Emotional Purity

All of this brings us to a concept that needs to be introduced to parents, taught to kids, and embraced by the entire family. The concept is "emotional purity."

In 2001, author Heather Paulson literally wrote the book on the subject. In her book, *Emotional Purity*, Paulson defines emotional intimacy as "a close, private relationship that would invoke strong feelings, passions, and the senses."[1] In contrast, emotional purity would be the ongoing discipline of not allowing your heart to go places it is not ready to go. It is following Solomon's bride's advice to not awaken love until you are ready for it.

Paulson says it this way: "I see emotional purity as the root of physical purity. The more emotionally connected you are with someone, the more you (desire) physical connection. Once a couple begins to attach emotionally, physical affection is naturally going to follow."[2]

Any commitment to sexual purity (think True Love Waits) is useless if there is not first and foremost a commitment to emotional purity.

My own life is a testimony to the connection between emotional and sexual purity. I can remember being taught by good parents and in a good youth ministry that sexual activity was reserved for marriage. I can remember clearly while still in middle school my youth pastor teaching that the greatest gift I could give my future spouse was my purity. I heard it, believed it, and was fully committed to that end. We didn't have purity rings back in that day, but I would have proudly worn one.

In 7th grade, I was fully committed to purity. In 8th grade...I was still in. By 9th grade, I was even to the point of looking down with "holier than thou" condemnation on those I knew that were being promiscuous in their relationships.

In 10th grade, I got a serious girlfriend and something significant changed in me. Suddenly, my purity commitment was entirely forgotten. The faithful desire to honor God with my body was fully and completely trumped by my emotional affections for my girlfriend. While there were certain physical lines I was committed to not crossing, I know that the relationship was far from God-honoring.

Was there conflict within me? Of course. Those high school years were some of the most tumultuous in my Christian life. Unfortunately, my desire for holy living and Christian obedience didn't stop me from becoming physical in ways that I know were sinful. Looking back, I am sure that my dilemma was, at its root, not a physical intimacy problem but one of emotional intimacy. Had I guarded my heart closer, my pre-marriage relationships would have never gotten physical.

This is how I coach my kids today. We have far more discussions in our house about emotional purity than sexual purity. Ultimately, it dictates much on our family's guidelines for dating and boy/girl relationships.

Many parents do well to tell their kids to "just say no" to sexual activity. However, we must admit that this will be near impossible if we encourage our kids to participate in a dating system by the same rules as the world. Specifically, if they are already emotionally connecting to others, we can't expect them to not get physically connected.

Many ultra-conservative authors and teachers have championed the need for emotional purity. For many, it is synonymous with the "courtship" movement that has gained momentum in the past twenty years. While I am neither advocating nor criticizing a courtship model, I am suggesting that we take an honest look at what tends to happen when young lovers get emotionally entwined. Even those in the mainstream can see the powerful implications of "giving your heart away" too many times and the long-term affect it will have on future relationships (particularly marriage).

My favorite music video of all time is by Gnarls Barkley. A filmmaker took their song *"Who's Gonna Save My Soul"*[3] and made a powerful little short film out of it. The first few minutes show a couple sitting in a café. It is obvious from the first few seconds that she is breaking up with him. She is explaining the "it's not you, it's me" garbage that break-ups are traditionally known for.

As the girl is talking, the guy is not fully engaged in what she is saying. He is too busy getting an extra plate and taking a butter knife and stabbing himself in the heart (it is pretty gory). He then reaches into his chest "Temple of Doom" style, pulls out his heart, and puts it on the plate in front of him. He slides it over to her and says: *"For you."*

She responds by saying: *"You do realize I'm breaking up with you, right?"*

The guy then gives a prophetic and true monologue: *"Well, that's the strange thing: it's actually yours now (his heart). I don't know why*

40

it works this way, but I'm never going to be able to get over you, so from now on, every other girl that I meet will be meticulously compared to you and, unfortunately, none of them will be able to measure up to the false memory of what you and I once had."

She responds: *"Maybe I can just keep it for a little while…and then eventually I'll give it back to you when we both find somebody new."*

He continues: *"Unfortunately, it won't work that way. Now that you have my heart, I'm pretty much an empty cavity inside. For lack of a better term: I'm 'heartless.' I will now treat each woman I meet with a passive/aggressive contentiousness that will ruin relationship after relationship for many years to come."*

Their expressions at the end of the conversation suggest that they both know it's true. It's pretty powerful stuff for a music video.

Helping Our Kids to Guard Their Hearts

Because these heart issues are so clearly in front of us, and their long-term impact is so obvious, parents must embrace their responsibility in helping to guide and protect their kids from the "serial dating" so prevalent in our culture. While I am not advocating an extreme, legalistic position as some do, I want to challenge parents to consider what their role is in guiding their kids to not carelessly give their hearts away before they are mature enough to handle the emotional and physical dimensions of a relationship. This is a critical role of parents that many have ignored.

We can see an illustration of the way God gives His people this same type of covering and protection in the writings of one of the Old Testament prophets. In Ezekiel 16, God gives him a story to tell about how He has cared for his people. It goes something like this:

A baby is born in secret and then abandoned in a field. The baby girl is left alone to die; unfed and uncared for, writhing around in a pool of blood. God saw that the baby was unloved and alone and had intense pity for her. From that moment, God took responsibility for her life and her well-being, speaking life and blessings on her, just as a good parent naturally does. The story goes on that the girl eventually matured sexually. The Bible says that her breasts were formed and her hair grew long and beautiful, yet she was still naked.

41

Then I love what is described in verse 8: *"Later I passed by, and when I looked at you and saw that you were old enough for love, I spread the corner of my garment over you and covered your naked body."*

God models for parents the kind of care and protection that our kids need. When their bodies begin to mature and their hearts begin to awaken to love, our children need safeguarding, not unbridled freedom to explore their new awareness. As these new emotions begin to stir within our kids, there are a few practical ways that we can provide a covering of protection for them.

First of all, emotional purity is an issue that parents would be wise to begin talking about sooner than they think they need to. If our kids know what to look for and expect in their hearts before it hits them, they will be more prepared to deal with it. A great book to read with the youngest of girls is Jennie Bishop's *The Princess and the Kiss.* This was regular required reading at our house.

Secondly, we must be prepared to turn feelings of attraction that our kids might have into teachable moments. Never label God-given recognition of the opposite-sex as "bad." Instead, we should turn the affections that are stirring in our kids into conversations. Ask: "What do you like about him or her? What types of qualities does that person have that you might look for in a spouse one day?"

Third, we should be mindful of our kids' friends and their perspectives and values regarding the opposite-sex. If my daughter's friends are all of a "boy crazy" mindset, I shouldn't be surprised if my daughter gets caught up in it as well. I'm not suggesting that all those friendships should immediately end, but I need to prepare her for the inevitability that our family is going to operate by a different set of values than most everybody else. Unfortunately, the "everybody else" we are different from might be others within the faith community.

Finally, as the growing, maturing heart of a teenager has a greater and greater desire to connect emotionally, strive to push them into a deeper emotional relationship with Christ. God has placed in each of His followers a longing to know Himself. Sadly, many of us fail to look to Christ to fill our deepest needs. Instead, we look to others to meet our needs for love, security, and self-worth. This is particularly true for teenagers. Wise parents will realize that one of their most important jobs is to teach their kids how to find and know their identity in Christ. Robert McGee's classic book *The Search for Significance* covers a Christian's identity in Christ better than anything else I have found.

While emotional purity is harder to define than physical purity, it is just as critical in helping our kids to be prepared for marriage one day. Parents must believe that and begin to act on it. Again, we wouldn't give plutonium to a preschooler. She simply does not have the maturity and understanding to know what she is dealing with. In the same way, we shouldn't encourage young people who are just awakening to brand new emotions to explore them without close parental guidance. Even though they may not know it, our kids desperately need us in this way.

five

Excuses

You might need to figure out why it's so hard
for you to talk about this stuff.

As I write this, my ultimate goal is to inspire and motivate each of us as parents to start engaging our kids in conversations about some critical issues. The hope is that doing so will ultimately help them to experience God's very best in their long-term marriage relationships.

These conversations and principles are not "formulas" that guarantee that "if we do things this way, then our kids will be forever free from the struggles that others encounter." There have been many formulaic parenting philosophies offered by well-meaning Christian teachers and authors over the years that have not provided the results they promised. It's not because their prescriptive formulas were wrong; it's just because the Christian life (and particularly parenting) is unpredictable. Parents must be careful not to extend to their children a plan for finding a mate that follows arbitrary rules while ignoring the leadership of the Holy Spirit in their lives. There is not a "one size fits all" paradigm.

If there were a formula for these things, we would plug our kids into it and never talk to God. We would trust the formula instead of daily depending on Him. That's never a good idea.

We have seen too many kids raised in carefully structured environments by well-intentioned parents who committed themselves to one formulaic approach. Often, these kids leave the house and gain a little freedom, only to reject their parent's faith outright. It is not unheard of for them to choose promiscuity, homosexuality, or another obvious rebellion against the way they were raised. You can find story after story online of young adults in their late 20's who are just now experiencing God's grace after being raised in an overly oppressive and shame-filled home.

Still, that does not describe the typical Christian family. Most exist on the other extreme, giving no leadership or direction whatsoever to their kids regarding relationships. What I am advocating is a shift for most families from the extreme of careless, no-holds-barred dating and back to a rational, intentional, scriptural middle.

What is Holding You Back?

The responsibility of communicating these realities clearly falls upon the shoulders of a child's parents. Still, many look for someone else to carry this burden. This might describe you. When you even contemplate talking openly about sexual issues with your kids, you become paralyzed and unable to move forward. Sadly, the biggest obstacle to talking with your kids is you.

Your discomfort. Your anxiety. Your past.

Why are parents reluctant to talk about sex with their kids? There are a number of possibilities. The more you can identify with, the more you might need to passionately seek God's power and restoration to enable you to do what does not come naturally for any of us.

1. Nobody Modeled it For You

For many of us, our parents left us to figure things out for ourselves and we have absolutely zero knowledge about how to have these conversations with our own kids. Given that our parents' generation didn't have many of the books and resources that we have today, this is probably true for many of us.

Unlike our parents, we are the most resourced and equipped generation in the history of the world. There are good books on just about every aspect of parenting. If you don't know what to say or how to say it, a little research and a little preparation will go a long way.

Maybe you are reluctant because you are afraid of even uttering some key words to your children. These are words you don't usually use in conversation, so speaking them to your kids with a straight face may be difficult. It might be a good idea to practice a bit.

Seriously. Get with you spouse and say out loud some of the words that you know will come up in conversations about sex and dating. Here are a few suggestions:

Sex. Intercourse. Penis. Vagina. Breast. Erection. Oral Sex. Masturbation. Period. Wet Dream.

Sure, it's a bit awkward, but it will get easier the more you do it. Maybe. But even if it does not, we still have to be grown-ups and get busy talking about this stuff. We could use other, more slang terms for body parts, but most experts who are smarter than I am recommend using anatomically correct words. I don't think the world will end if you say "wee-wee" instead of "penis," but that's what the experts tend to suggest. You would be wise to seek God on this and use your own best judgment for your particular situations.

> *Jenifer's Perspective:*
> *"Yes, talking about these things is scary. I am scared every time I do it. But we cannot ignore our responsibility just because it is scary or uncomfortable."*

2. You Are Afraid to Take Away Their Innocence

Parents are generally not in a hurry to see their kids grow up, so they are typically reluctant to introduce information of a sexual nature to their kids. After all, why should we rush to take away their innocence? This is a concern for many parents, particularly those whose oldest children are still rather young. That's because guarding the innocence of our firstborns is usually far easier than guarding the innocence of our younger children. With five kids in my home and an age span of fifteen years, there has been a vast difference between what my first-born was aware of at ten years old and my fourth-born was aware of at the same age. We haven't set out to expose our younger kids to "adult" issues, but they end up hearing them talked about by their older siblings in the normal operation of our home.

No matter how old your kids are, one thing is for certain: they will be exposed to far more "mature" issues than you think. You can and should be diligent to protect them, but there are just too many opportunities for them to encounter the world's perspective on these things. Even if you don't have TVs and your kids are homeschooled and your family only uses the internet to watch old video clips of Psalty the Singing Songbook, your kids will still be exposed to things that you cannot control. I have personally come to believe that children have internal antennae in their heads that receive information directly from MTV.

Parents who are passionately committed to ensuring that their kids have a long, carefree childhood should be applauded. Pursue that goal with diligence. However, do not prioritize the short-term goal of innocence over the long-term goal of helping them to pursue a lifetime of purity. In a similar way, do not equate giving clear information on human relationships and sexuality with taking away their innocence. Sure, hearing about the details of sexual intercourse for the first time will freak them out, but it will not ruin their lives. In contrast, growing up unprepared for the challenges they might face sexually has the power to do just that.

3. You Can't Relate To These Struggles

Maybe you are reluctant because you can't personally relate to any of this. You were completely pure growing up and never even considered stepping outside of God's boundaries regarding your personal sexuality. You saved yourself completely for marriage and cannot imagine anyone who loves Jesus doing otherwise.

If that description fits, congratulations! You are a shining example of purity! However, you cannot assume that your kids' experience will be like yours. If you do, you are being naïve. Actually, the word naïve would probably be the understatement of the millennium.

There may be, of course, a few exceptions to this, but as a general rule, our kids are living in a far different world than the one we grew up in. The culture has changed, the pressures have changed, and our kids are facing a full-court press from the enemy. We may not have had any problem saving ourselves sexually for marriage, but chances are (and statistics suggest) that our kids WILL have problems pulling that feat off. We won't know until we talk about it with them.

More naïve parents may also wrongly assume that their kids aren't ready yet. While this may be true for some, parents should know that our children are being exposed to far more information at a younger age than any generation before. This cannot be ignored.

4. You Feel Like a Hypocrite

You may be reluctant because of your own past failures in this area. You don't feel credible enough to speak with authority on what your kids should know and do. Even reading about the long-term effects of being careless with our hearts and our sexuality stirs up a variety of powerful emotions in you. We absolutely cannot allow these feelings to stop us from moving forward with our children. If we are silent or passive, we are setting our children up to repeat our mistakes. In a very practical way, this is the clearest manifestation of a "generational curse," something the Bible warns us against time and time again. Whether we believe in such things or not, we certainly don't want the junk from our past to negatively affect our children's futures.

Know this for certain: the enemy wants you to feel inadequate and paralyzed. He wants you to remain silent.

God has the power to break those chains, but it definitely will not come through silence. This is addressed in greater detail in chapter 22. If you have experienced significant hurt and brokenness from your past decisions (and have not been adequately restored), then there would be value in skipping ahead to that chapter before moving on.

Another dimension related to our failures is that we are wary of broaching these subjects with our teenagers for fear that they will ask us specific questions about our past. They might ask blunt, intrusive questions like "Did you have sex before marriage?" If you choose to be completely honest and transparent, they might come to the conclusion that you made some bad choices when you were young and you turned out okay, so what's the big deal?

I would recommend handling this much the way that renowned Bible teacher Beth Moore has handled it over the years. In her teaching, she often makes reference to some incredibly significant past hurts in her life, but she never goes into detail. She typically summarizes them in broad terms, choosing to focus more on the impact that they had on her life and the brokenness she was left with. She then draws the greatest attention to the restorative and redemptive power of Christ. This accomplishes at least two things: it doesn't allow people to fixate on whatever hurt she encountered and it turns people back to Jesus as the only one who can set things right.

In the same way, you don't ever have to feel obligated to dredge up all the specifics of your past. Instead, you can simply share that you have some significant regrets that you wish you could go back and do differently. As appropriate, you can also share that you did not, in fact, turn out okay. You have wounds and hurts from the broken nature of your past that God is still in the process of making right. This takes time and, honestly, all of us are works in progress.

You would be wise to regularly ask God for clear discernment regarding the nature of any hypocrisy you might feel. It is always possible that you want to avoid the subject altogether because your own sex life is currently a mess. Dysfunction in any couple's married life makes these issues distasteful and the easy option is to choose to simply not talk about them. If that is the case, you should get whatever help you need to move toward wholeness and to keep your kids' needs at the front of your consciousness. Your kids require parents who will provide the guidance they so desperately need, even if you don't have it all together. But don't be satisfied with dysfunction. We should all be constantly seeking direction from God and others to move toward sexual wholeness and purity in our current relationships.

Take a minute for a little personal contemplation. If any of these concerns sound familiar, there is a great likelihood that you could be in knots over this issue. Again, remember that we have a God who is ready, willing, and able to help us face these challenges head-on. Always remember that *"the one who is in you is greater than the one who is in the world."* (I John 4:4) It is never a bad idea to link arms with your spouse, a good friend, or someone else who can encourage you to press forward into these "talks" with your kids. You can know that the Holy Spirit of God is always with you to give guidance and help.

What to Expect from the Rest of This Book

Hopefully, you are beginning to feel a conviction that, as parents, we need to become more intentional in leading and guiding our children through the rocky waters of their budding sexuality. However, inspiration can quickly lose steam if there isn't a clear direction to walk. We need a plan.

The next fifteen chapters are some suggested "talks" to have with your kids along the way. Some are obvious, but others might represent an issue that you may have never considered. Because every family is different, there isn't a rigid, clearly defined age to broach each topic. There will occasionally be general suggestions, but they are not hard and fast rules. Follow God's leading on this, but remember that your kids need to hear your authoritative spin on these things before they hear it from someone else.

Each chapter will include some background information on the issue that will hopefully provide enough relevant detail to launch a conversation. Then things will get practical. There is a **"How to Talk About _____"** at the end of each of the next fifteen chapters. It is there to give a few ideas about getting the conversations started. I attribute this section in each chapter to Jenifer. Whenever I prepare to preach or teach, I often hear her tell me: "That sounds great in theory, but how do we do it? How do we live that truth out in a practical and specific way?" It is my prayer that the coaching given will help you to turn normal conversations in your home into teachable moments.

While these topics and resources might serve as tools to get you talking about some critical subjects, do not see them as an exhaustive checklist of things to cover. Likewise, do not think that once a subject is addressed in a moment of conversation that the work is done. Guiding our kids through these issues might require dozens of conversations. Hundreds of "talks." Wise parents will reinforce perspectives while watching TV, in seeing current events unfold, through homework assignments and in a million other ways. The dialogue can and should be ongoing.

The chapters ahead are all over the map and there isn't a strict order in which to read them. Either tackle them one by one or start with the ones that are already hot issues within your home and situation. The key is to get comfortable talking about this stuff in your home.

You can do it. I promise. With God's help and guidance, you can do it.

Part Two:
Fifteen Conversations
Your Family Must Have
Sooner Than You Think

six

The Opposite Sex

Dating Principles to Start Teaching Your Preschooler

There is a small pond in our neighborhood, probably no bigger than a few acres. It has a healthy population of fish that the neighborhood kids catch and release.

I would imagine that the existence of a fish living in that pond is a relatively simple and peaceful one. He has a limited understanding of reality. He swims. He eats. He reproduces. He has never laid eyes on a mountain or skyscraper or a sectional sofa. His tiny little brain has no understanding of philosophy or ethics or taxes. Except for the occasional kid who puts a hook in his mouth, stares at him for a few moments and then tosses him back in the water, he has very little stress.

What would it be like to be able to "speak fish" for a few minutes and try to explain to a large mouth bass in that pond that there exists a whole different world beyond the environment of his watery home? How easy would it be for me to convince him that there are trillions upon trillions of creatures who successfully live in the open air that he can't seem to breathe? Outside the pond, there is history and culture and art and beauty on display in millions of different dimensions and colors. There are digital cameras and drive-thru restaurants and reality television shows.

If I could somehow speak "fish," it is unlikely that he would believe me about any of this. In fact, he would probably not even have the ability to comprehend what I was trying to describe for him. It would be too far removed from his understanding of what is real and what is true.

Our kids are a lot like that fish.

The everyday environment in which our young people grow up will help define, in a large part, their perspective of the world. It will determine for them what is normal, what is acceptable, and what is expected of them. The value systems and behaviors that they observe will play a significant part in creating their worldview.

If a particular lifestyle or belief is prevalent in their world and it seems to work for the people around them, they are likely to embrace it as their own. It becomes the lens through which they see the world. From that point on, it is unlikely that they will easily see it any other way.

Psychologists define this as a person's "schema." Webster defines "schema" as "a mental codification that includes a particular organized way of perceiving cognitively and responding to a complex situation or set of stimuli."[1] This is a fancy way of saying that a person's experiences and background will cause them to think about things and issues a certain way. Dictionary.com puts it this way: "A schema provides the basis by which someone relates to the events he or she experiences."[2]

Before we discuss the goal of helping our children develop a healthy perspective of the opposite-sex and what dating relationships might look like, a more foundational place to start would be to ask the following question: "Should the schema of a Christ-follower be different from the schema of someone whose life is not submitted to Christ?" In other words, should their values and perspectives and worldview be different?

We would think so.

However, it is becoming increasingly difficult in western Christianity to see a difference between believers and unbelievers.

The line separating us with regard to our worldview, our habits, and our lifestyle choices is becoming more and more grey. It is an understatement to suggest that, like the church of Laodicea mentioned in Revelation 3:14-21, we have become lukewarm. We blend in pretty well with the world around us.

I am not suggesting that Christians everywhere should band together, isolate themselves on an island and commit to a strict moral code that, ultimately, nobody can possibly adhere to. What I am suggesting is that Christ-followers must constantly strive to find the balance of being in the world but to not operate like the world. Sadly, in our attempts to be "relevant," many people in the church have lost sight of that completely.

In John 15:19, Jesus put it this way: *"If you belonged to the world, it would love you as its own. As it is, you do not belong to the world, but I have chosen you out of the world. That is why the world hates you."* Jesus made clear that one of the facets of being His disciples would be that the world, as a whole, wouldn't like us. It wouldn't fully understand us. In contrast, He says that if we are of the world (as opposed to being of Him), then we will fit into the dominant culture very nicely.

As Christian families, we should be consistently driving home the truth that we are called to be and live and think differently than the world. We must train our kids very early on that we are not going to play by the world's rules. We do this not to be restrictive but because God has called us to a better way.

It may be hard sometimes. We may end up feeling a bit like fish out of water, but it's just the reality of living as a Christ-follower in a fallen world.

Why is This Relevant to The Opposite Sex?

While our kids are living in the world, they will be exposed to a wide variety of world-views that are radically different than what Christ has called us to be. With regards to the issue of what dating should look like, young teenagers whose parents have not been deliberate to define a few rules and realities will naturally come to embrace what they see around them. In their young minds, what the world offers to them will be normal, reasonable, and appropriate. However, those who are raised in homes with intentional parents will already know both some perspectives and some parameters regarding what they can expect in their interactions with the opposite-sex. They will have been equipped from a very early age to consider that some of the culture's ideas on this subject are just plain wrong. Some of them are even potentially dangerous.

This sentiment is captured perfectly in Proverbs 14:12: *"There is a way that appears to be right, but in the end it leads to death."* That's some pretty dramatic language, but it does remind wise believers that much of what our world practices as normal behavior is severely skewed and even badly broken.

I believe this definitely applies to typical teen dating behaviors. With clear evidence found in the horrific divorce rate and with rampant sexual sin in both married adults and young people, we cannot assume that our current western system is working. Wise parents will both realize this and then be deliberate to equip their kids accordingly.

Because we are called by Christ to be different, there must be an understanding in our homes that even if everybody else is doing something one way, we may choose to operate by an entirely different set of rules. That is simply a non-negotiable component of being Christ-followers. When talking to our kids, this is always a great place to insert an illustration about everybody jumping off a cliff. Kids just love that one!

We must get the basic expectation of being different from the world firmly established in the minds of each person in our families. Our family philosophy of dating, and in an even broader sense, our family's philosophy of how our kids will interact with the opposite-sex in general, will lay the foundation for many of the issues we are unpacking in the forthcoming chapters.

Exactly what that looks like for each particular family is not for me to decide. Again, there are no arbitrary rules for every home. There are plenty of books out there that seem to offer "God's exact plan for dating." I am very skeptical of these. Instead of looking for that ever-elusive formula, it is our responsibility as parents to prayerfully seek God's leadership regarding how it will look in each of our unique situations.

There are many topics that need to be discussed with our kids far sooner than we think, but this one is critical. In many ways, it is the foundation that everything else is built upon. Establishing early some guidelines for interacting with the opposite-sex will give our kids from their earliest memories an idea of how things will work once they get older. The earlier we start, the better.

As a "best case scenario," beginning these discussions when our kids are far away from any interest in the opposite-sex is ideal. For here is the mistake that most parents make: they do not start setting parameters on dating until their kids start exploring their first relationship. If a young teen is already there and her parents start dropping rules on her for the first time, it may get ugly.

I had a friend who used to say, "If you don't define reality, someone else will define reality for you." That is why it is not a bad idea for us to begin considering guidelines for dating while our kids are still in diapers. If we don't begin to show our kids at a very early age what will be normal in our homes, when they begin to notice the opposite-sex, they are likely to assume that their rules of engagement are identical to everybody else's. Why wouldn't they? If we haven't defined their reality, then they will naturally assume that what they see around them is right for them, as well. Any new restrictions that are introduced for the first time once our kids have already "turned the corner" are likely to be met with frustration and rebellion.

Try taking a fish out of a pond for a few minutes and see how it does. We can be assured that it will not be happy.

Wise parents will start laying some general ground rules for dating when their kids are very young so that it is built into their normal "schema." Then, when they grow up, they won't be shocked.

How to Talk About the Opposite Sex

There will be a long list of potential conversations about sex and relationships we will have with our kids over the years. Though these talks will rarely feel completely comfortable and fluid, the earlier we start, the more natural they should feel. From their earliest days, it is recommended that we begin articulating a few key guidelines that characterize how "we are going to approach this differently than most people." Where does that begin? Let me offer a few suggestions.

1. Don't Do "Cooties"

With even the youngest of children, how we characterize the opposite-sex has the potential to set the pace for much of their young lives. The principle that should drive us, therefore, should not be that boys are gross and that girls have "cooties." Doing that can be dangerous, because one day our kids will grow up. They will realize that they have a powerful interest in the other gender and they may come to see our opinion as unreliable. After all, if I tell my son that girls are a boring waste of time but then he later begins to notice that they smell good and have nice curvy parts that are curiously attractive, he may not trust my opinion on these matters in the future.

On the other hand, if a parent characterizes the opposite-sex as very different, a bit confusing, but uniquely wonderful, the child may not fully believe it at the time. But later on, when their eyes are opened and their God-given sexuality begins to blossom, it will affirm what he or she has come to suspect. "I previously didn't believe Mom and Dad about this," they will reason, "but maybe they were on to something."

I have always liked giving young people the analogy of Liquid Drano to describe the other gender in general and sex in particular. If a sink is clogged, Drano is incredible stuff. It has an amazing purpose and it works wonders. However, it can also be very harmful and poisonous if it is not used properly. The truth is that it is possible for something to be both wonderful and dangerous at the same time. It's all in how it is handled.

In the same way, it's important to characterize the opposite-sex as pretty awesome. Point out their valuable and worthwhile characteristics, even with the youngest of kids. When you sense that your teenager has noticed someone, encourage him to talk about her. "That girl is pretty special. She seems to stand out in some way. What do you think makes her so unique?"

2. Don't Set a Firm Age for When Your Kids Can Date

This is one of those areas where I cannot provide every parent of every kid with a formulaic age to begin dating. I have not found in Scripture nor determined from experience a crystal-clear age when it is appropriate. Because of that, I do not recommend that we give our kids a strict benchmark like "when you are sixteen." However, I do like the sentiment expressed by the young people of the YouTube channel "Blimeycow" in their *Seven Tips for Successful Dating* video. "Tip #1: If you are thirteen, you are disqualified."[3] It suggests that most kids expect to get started way too early.

In addition, a strict line like that is full of potential disastrous complications. Telling a boy who is 15 years and 11 months old that he cannot have a girlfriend and then a month later telling him he can (and giving him keys to the car) is too much freedom preceded by too little practice. Not much good will come of that.

> *Jenifer's Perspective:*
> *"While we avoid giving a recommended age that parents should allow their kids to have boyfriends and girlfriends, it is never a bad idea to delay it as long as possible so they can grow and mature."*

While there may not be a firm recommended age where every teenager should be given the green light to begin dating, one study clearly makes the argument that it is wise to put it off as long as possible. This is especially if we desire to help our kids to remain sexually (and even emotionally) pure leading into marriage. Researchers have found a shocking correlation between the age that dating begins and the percentage of those who had sex before graduation.

Turn the page for some truly eye-opening data that has serious ramifications for our kids and when they start to "date."

Age Began Dating	% Who Had Sex Before Graduation
12	91%
13	56%
14	53%
15	40%
16	20%[4]

The takeaway: we are free to encourage our 6th or 7th grade sons to have girlfriends and to let them "date" within the context of our homes. We have every right to drive our 13-year-old daughters to the movies with their "boyfriends." It seems innocent enough; but don't be naïve about this research. We can assume that this won't happen to our kids, but the evidence strongly suggests that the earlier a kid starts dating, the more likely he or she is to become sexually active. Blindly sticking our heads in the sand and insisting that our kids are different and that they will somehow beat the odds is irresponsible in light of the data.

3. Establish Some Criteria for How You Will Know Your Kids Might Be Ready to Date

If we are not giving our children a specific target age of when dating and relationships might be an option for them, what do we tell them? I would recommend that we tell them that we are looking for certain key markers of maturity in their lives.

One marker will be that they are finding their personal identity in Christ far more than in their peers. If God is setting their standard for relationships and for purpose in life, relationships with the opposite-sex can be explored with the confidence that we are not making them out to be more than they were meant to be.

Another marker will be that they handle their other relationships with maturity. Young people whose relationships with family and friends are characterized by selfishness will be prone to bring the same attitude into any dating relationship. This is a bad habit to learn in early dating experiences. If it is practiced frequently enough, a core drive of selfishness can be easily carried into marriage.

A final marker will be that they can manage a "break-up" without being emotionally devastated. Of course, the end of a relationship can and will be painful, but one sign of spiritual and emotional maturity in a young person is that she will see her circumstances within the context of God's sovereign work in her life. Being hurt is one thing. Being sick for months with emotional grief is another.

When they are young, we need to communicate to our kids that, if and when we see appropriate signs of maturity in both them and the person they want to "go out with," there will still be some clearly defined rules for "dating." I would recommend that most interaction take place in your home. A good parameter to set would be that they will not be allowed to go off alone on a date until there is an extraordinary level of trust established between both the parents and the kids who are dating, as evidenced by some of the spiritual and emotional maturity markers mentioned above.

> *Jenifer's Perspective:*
> *"As for dating away from home—dances, parties, movies, etc.—it is wise to do it in a group setting. Encourage your kids to think of their peers and siblings as modern day chaperones."*

All this may sound like a lot of ground to cover while our kids are still in elementary school, but there is no harm in defining these parameters early on. On the other hand, there is plenty of drama, conflict, and potential emotional harm waiting for those parents who don't start talking about the opposite-sex until their kids want to start dating. This will happen to the vast majority of parents who are passive in this area.

But I might be wrong. Your kids might be so extraordinary that they are the ones who defy the odds. Your thoughts of "that won't happen to my kids" might be spot on. It's just that this is the thinking of just about every parent I encounter. Unfortunately, we can't all be right.

There are, of course, a few exceptions. There are the few parents who, when their daughter gets pregnant, loudly exclaim, "I knew this would happen! I saw it coming!" But for the rest of us who are not on the stage of the Jerry Springer show, this is not the case. We can go on assuming that our kids will quickly pass through puberty and easily transition into relational maturity without any up-front coaching from their parents. However, we will likely have significant regrets later on.

I, for one, do not want to be a parent who allows a world that doesn't care about the welfare of my kids to define for them what is normal as they explore these critical areas of life. Despite my many shortcomings, I want to remain committed, with God's help, to diligently paint for them a picture of how they can appreciate, honor, and interact with the opposite-sex in guarded ways as they get older. But I must get started long before they get there.

seven

BIRDS AND BEES

The Talk That Nobody Wants to Talk About

I have a vague childhood memory of the day I learned the truth about sex. I remember my mom walking into my room at bedtime and sitting down at the foot of my bed. She had a serious look on her face. I didn't know if I was in trouble or if someone had died, or what. I just knew something important was happening. I think I was about nine.

It was at that moment that I experienced what most of us would refer to as "the talk." I don't remember the details, but I am certain that it was the first time I learned the foundational truth that, for a woman to get pregnant, a man's penis had to go inside a woman's vagina. As with every other kid in the history of mankind, I can remember it totally freaking me out. Though I could almost believe that people would endure such a thing to have a baby, I was sure my mom was nuts when she suggested that married people experience this act regularly because they really enjoy it.

She went on to show me the set of four books she had in her lap. I think the title of the series had the words "Life Cycle" or something like that in them. They were about "changes" and had some basic "where babies come from" information. The books were hardback, red in color, and fit nicely into a cardboard sleeve. I can still remember them clearly, not only because I took the time to read them, but because I think that they stayed on a bookshelf at my parents' house until I was well into my 30's. I referred back to them now and again, just to review the fundamentals. (That was a joke.)

Looking back, I don't remember my mom being "stressed out" during the conversation, but I'm sure she was. No parent looks forward to having a talk that will, in many ways, draw to a close the innocence of their children. I have yet to meet a parent who takes this lightly. In fact, there are few things that give parents more anxiety than having "the talk."

In our heads, we realize that we have the responsibility of telling our kids about sex, but the prospect of doing so can scare us to death. The fear can tempt us to put it off until much later, which can get us into trouble. As a general rule, if the first time you broach this subject is as your daughter is climbing into the limo after her wedding reception, you probably waited too long.

As I talk to the parents of younger children, I am reminded of how overwhelming this subject can be. I am also convinced of how important it is: not just in terms of having a single conversation with a child, but in terms of the far greater task of helping our kids have a healthy, Biblical view of sexuality. As we have said before, the stakes are just too high for us to neglect this responsibility.

> *Jenifer's Perspective:*
> *"We must remember that this is not a one-time talk, but an ongoing dialogue. I want my kids to know that they can ask me anything. No question is a bad question. No subject is off limits."*

Corrie Ten Boom was five years old when she heard a word spoken by a man in anger as she walked down the street with her father. It was a strange utterance that she had never heard before, equivalent to what we would know today as the "f-word." She asked her father what the word meant. The father responded by asking her to carry his briefcase for him. She said, "It's too heavy." He then told her, "When you are older and stronger you can bear it. For now you must trust me to carry it for you."[1] The same was true for the word.

This father was wise not to expose his daughter to more than she could handle.

Parents today must prayerfully determine what our kids need to hear and when they need to hear it. Having the wisdom and sensitivity to know what is best in your unique situation might be the greatest challenge associated with sexual education in your family. It should push you to your knees before doing just about anything else in moving forward.

Know this for certain: our kids are exposed to more "adult information" via more avenues than we ever were. They will hear things from their friends at school, catch references on TV and on the internet, and even hear things mentioned in church that will make them curious (it's amazing how many questions a 6-year-old can ask after hearing just one Christmas Eve service reference to the fact that Mary never had sexual relations with a man).

A good guideline is that we should want our kids to hear details from us before they hear them from somewhere else. There is no perfect age, but many experts feel that detailed conversations between parent and child should be taking place by eight or nine. This may need to be younger for children attending schools with lots of foul-mouthed, obnoxious boys. It could be older for families who homeschool and are able to be more protective. Because every situation is unique, we should all seek Godly counsel regarding what age might be right for our children.

Talks about sexuality might begin when a child has simple questions as a preschooler and it should continue far into young adulthood. Perhaps the pressure might be relieved a bit if we see "the talk" as one key focal point in the process. Or it might add more pressure because we know that our job is never finished. Whatever the case, you would be wise to see this event as one small piece of a bigger picture. Your goal should not be to have a "talk." Your goal should be to prepare them for healthy married sexuality. This will require a lot of talks through the years.

I stress this to point out that we must become comfortable with this topic and it must be easily discussed in our homes. If our kids are hearing a regular dose of the world's tainted perspective, it's hard to pass on the truth that God created sex and that it must be honored and handled with great care. The more timid we are on this topic, the more generations we will raise up who experience defeat and frustration in their sexuality.

How To Talk About The Birds and The Bees

As you prepare to have this critical conversation, your heart will likely be filled with fear. In that moment, you must be courageous. Someone once said that courage is not the absence of fear, but it is choosing to act in spite of the fear. Walk in confidence knowing that God wants you to lovingly share this information with your children. More importantly, know that He is with you.

In the Years Leading Up to "The Talk"

How our children receive the message we give them about sex is, in many ways, closely tied to the positive foundation we lay in the years leading up to it. For those parents who feel that their children are not quite ready yet, there are several things that we can focus on.

First of all, we must be sure to model a healthy relationship in our marriages. The security we give our children will be greatly based upon the love that they sense between mom and dad. When the time comes to describe what happens in the sexual act, and we insist that it is a beautiful, wonderful act of love that mom and dad share, the confidence they have in our relationship may determine how they respond to our message. Even single parents can present this truth in the context of how God designed things to be.

Secondly, we must be diligent to protect our children's innocence. Unfortunately, there are a million different ways for our kids to get information about sex than from us. The average age of first-time exposure to pornography is getting younger every year. We must also give attention to the sexual awareness of our children's peers. Kids talk openly (and often with braggadocio) about what they know, so we must stay in good communication with other parents and our children's teachers about what they might be hearing. We cannot afford to be lazy in this area.

68

Third, parents should look for signs that their children are ready for "the talk." Some questions to consider include:

- What are their natural curiosities?
- What questions are they asking?
- What are they being exposed to outside the home?
- In addition to their chronological age, what is their emotional age? What can they handle?

Finally, parents must seek God's leadership in all aspects of parenting, but particularly as it relates to this specific conversation. While friends and family might provide us with some wisdom and encouragement, only God fully knows and understands the heart of each individual child. As Isaiah 30:21 says, only He can lead His disciples to hear His voice say, *"This is the way, walk in it."* We must ask God to give us conviction through His Holy Spirit regarding when we are to speak to our children about sex.

Having "The Talk"

There is no "silver bullet" process or solution for making this painless and stress-free, but there are some guidelines to consider.

1. Get prayed up. As the days lead up to your conversation, ask friends who know your family well to be interceding for you. You must trust that God WILL walk this out with you, preparing your child (His child) for what you will tell him or her.

2. Dads talk to sons; moms talk to daughters. While there are some cases where single parents may need to cross gender lines, a general rule should be that dads talk with sons and moms talk with daughters. Once the truth is out there and the ice has been broken, the other parent can share their perspective at a later date.

3. Practice before you preach. It helps if you talk out what you plan to say with your spouse or with another good friend. If possible, practice with someone who has already had the conversation with his or her kids. They may be a good source of advice regarding lessons learned and land mines to avoid.

4. Build it into a fun "coming of age" event. Our tradition is to take our kids on a road trip for a few days, building lots of "you're growing up" conversations into our time. "The talk" is included in the middle of many other things, as it is an essential thing that every young person needs to know.

5. Start talking. At some point, you have to jump in there and get the conversation started. It will feel awkward, but that's normal. To get the ball rolling, I always started with something like this: "As you get older, I need to tell you about something that every young man and woman needs to know. I've been praying about this and I think it's about time I told you."

6. Keep it age-appropriate. Strive to share some basic things, but you don't need to share everything at the front end. If the relationship is solid and you can make it comfortable for them, their deeper questions will continue to trickle in over time. Also, try not to be confusing with your language. If you tell your 6-year-old that Mommy has an egg inside of her, he will never look at an omelet the same way again.

7. Use available resources. There are a number of great tools out there to help parents through this process. Instead of providing a script here, I encourage you to seek out those resources. Steve Farrar's example in *Point Man* was very helpful for me. The bottom line is that you don't have to go it alone. These books are also a good idea because you can store them in a place where your kids can easily get to them. Encourage your kids to look at them on their own.

8. Be positive! Through everything you do, your goal is to communicate to your child that the sexual facet of humanity is a good thing. They may not believe it at first (in fact, they are likely to think you are absolutely crazy), but your reassurance that sex is wonderful will go a long way to giving them a good first-impression of it, even if they don't fully get it.

9. Ask for a response. A good question is: "What do you think about all this?" Don't be surprised or worried if the shock of the whole thing leads them to some quiet contemplation. One dad told me his son responded with, "I could have gone the rest of my life without hearing that."

10. Put everything in the right context: marriage. Though this is probably the first time they will have heard about sex, it most certainly will not be the last. Stress from the earliest point possible that God designed sexuality to be expressed exclusively between two people who are fully committed to one another. Anything less than that has the real potential to compromise relationships and cheapen true intimacy.

Once your kids are fully aware of this unique and bizarre thing that married people do to express their love for one another, it is important that you consistently put sex in a positive light. As your kids get older and are bombarded with the world's perspective of sex with no consequences, you might be tempted to counteract that message with another extreme that is equally unhealthy. Let me explain:

While many parents fail their kids by allowing them to explore relationships and their sexuality with no parameters, some parents fail them in another way. These well-meaning parents bombard their teenagers with a variety of messages that all say the same thing. "Sex is bad. Don't do it. It's dangerous. Those sexual feelings and desires are evil, so suppress them at all costs." These messages are both wrong and dangerous. Above anything else, the most important thing parents can communicate to their kids is that sex is an amazing gift from God. It is beautiful and should be celebrated and honored.

We have an unwritten rule at our house that we want to gross out our kids at least once a week by our shows of physical affection. While the thought of their parents being intimate may make their stomachs turn, it does affirm for them that intimacy is a highly valued part of our marriage relationship.

After The Talk

In the days (and even years) after having the talk, you need to make yourself available to discuss things further. Once you broach the subject and your child knows what happens during sex, you need to give them some time to process and to develop some questions. The key is to let them know that you will always tell them the truth. You should also inform your kids that their friends don't know anything and that you are a far better source of information than their peers are.

Difficult as it might seem, I want to assure every parent that they have what it takes to do this. Scary or uncomfortable as it may be, parents have stumbled through this conversation for thousands of years and our species has flourished. The fact that you are chewing on these issues in the context of this book proves that you are better prepared than the vast majority of parents out there. Jenifer and I would love to cheer you on (picture Will Ferrell's Spartan cheerleader sketches) to boldly tackle these issues at home and reject passivity as an option.

More than that, I encourage you to remember that there is a God who loves you, who loves your children, and who walks with you through all things. If He wants you to lovingly have this conversation with your kids (and He does), then when the time is right, He will be there to give you His peace and the right words to say. The awesome part of that is that I don't have to dress up like a cheerleader.

eight

Preparation

How to Look for a Spouse, Not Just a Date

Ask most teenagers in America what the purpose of dating is and they are likely to stare back at you with a confused expression. Try it out. Ask this seemingly innocuous question to your preteens and teenagers (What is the purpose of dating?) and see what sorts of answers they give. Most kids simply haven't given it much thought.

If they are pressed long enough about why teenagers date, they are likely to offer self-serving answers like "to have fun." They might even give answers of a pragmatic nature such as "to see what they like in the opposite-sex." For many older teens, the response that would immediately enter their minds would deal with having an outlet for their sex drive, but most would never dream of saying that out loud.

The tragedy is that if anything of significance is not done with purpose, it is likely to be a careless pursuit that ultimately distracts from the will of God for our lives. This includes teens and their dating relationships. If young people do not learn to approach opposite-sex relationships and dating with clear purpose and intention, the result will often be one of significant pain and suffering. Not only will they miss out on the positives that purposeful dating might offer them, they will be distracted from the very thing that matters most in life: finding full satisfaction in a relationship with Christ.

At its foundation, most would agree that the purpose of dating (or other forms of courtship) is to identify a marriage partner. Up until recent history, most in our culture understood that. When a young man was ready for marriage, he would begin to deliberately pursue a girl who caught his eye or whose personality captured his heart. They would spend time together (date) and eventually decide if they were willing to commit themselves in marriage. If they were, there would be a proposal. If not, there would eventually be a break up. It was not unlike what happens today, but the difference is that this process is taking place with younger and younger people who are so far removed from being ready for marriage that the purpose for dating is completely lost.

One thing remains true: young people want to date. They want to have a boyfriend/girlfriend. They have God-given desires that lead them to want to connect with the opposite-sex. What most young people fail to realize is that being in an exclusive relationship with one person is rarely an effective means to help identify what one likes or doesn't like in a possible mate. Young couples in relationships are typically thinking most about how the other person makes them feel, not about the other person's well being, internal character or Christian commitment. Sadly, these feelings will often cover up issues of substance.

Instead of teenagers growing up with a view of dating as an end in itself, I recommend that parents begin to train their kids to intentionally start looking for a spouse, not just a date-to carefully watch the people around them to determine what they will value most in a future mate. Kids can learn from even their elementary school years that there is great value in observing their opposite-sex friends and the married couples that they know. Being intentional in this can make boyfriends and girlfriends an unnecessary component of the young to mid-teen years.

The sooner we can give our kids an understanding of the purpose of dating, the better. We must help them to see that our approach to dating might be different than most of their peers. If they begin to embrace this, they will notice very early on a significant contrast between their family's approach and just about everyone else's.

If the reason to date is to find a spouse, a parent can begin to make the argument that dating should be put off until the season of life when they are ready to pursue marriage. They can explain the basic truth that maintaining sexual purity within a long-term relationship is a near impossibility for most people. There are, therefore, good reasons to delay things as long as practically possible.

In the meantime, we can take advantage of every teachable moment possible to help our kids to learn something about the people around them. If they embrace the fact that God has an amazing plan for them to find the perfect person that they can commit themselves to for life, they can begin to relax, trusting Him to bring things about in His own time. However, it doesn't mean that they have to sit on the bench while everyone else plays the field. They just need to be a bit more strategic.

From the time their friends started "dating," we have encouraged our kids to observe what their friends' relationships are like. Because they aren't personally in the relationship, they are able to critically examine things without an emotional bias. Their conclusions have typically been that what their peers are doing is pretty pointless.

Just because a boy begins to notice girls, it doesn't mean that he has to make it his objective to immediately have a girlfriend. The desire may be there, but it doesn't have to be acted on in the immediate future. As his parents, we don't want to suppress it, but instead to shift his energy into beginning to figure out what to look for in a wife. This is where some significant parental coaching comes in play.

How to Talk About Preparing for Marriage

How can you begin to help your kids think long-term? How do you help them to start looking for characteristics they might desire in a spouse instead of focusing only on the short-term goal of finding someone to date?

This requires sensitivity (a Holy Spirit-led sixth sense) on your behalf to pick up on when your teen is beginning to take an interest in someone. It will likely come at about the same time that they begin to notice the opposite-sex, in general. They may get weird, act shy, or be constantly looking for chances to be with the object of their affection. When you notice behaviors like this, your goal should not be to embarrass him or her but to be a part of the conversation. You can start by helping him or her to realize that those feelings and observations are okay. In fact, they are God-birthed.

> *Jenifer's Perspective:*
> *"Realize that our goal as parents should be to affirm their natural interest in the opposite-sex. We must be careful not to demonize it."*

We need to let our kids know that our job as parents is to help them to navigate their feelings and to help them to learn something in the process. It is also our responsibility to keep them guarded from rushing into something for which they are not yet ready. Specifically, we hope that they learn to identify what they are looking for in a spouse by observing the people around them. When one of my kids begins to notice the opposite-sex, it is the perfect opportunity for me to ask good questions: "What do you like about him or her? What would it be like to be married to someone like that someday? What about him/her might begin to annoy you after a while?"

Beyond these general questions, there are some things you can help them to look for that will serve them well in their eventual pursuit of a marriage partner. While someone's appearance will typically be the first thing that makes your young teenager notice someone, you should teach early on that physical beauty has the power to attract, but it doesn't have the power to sustain a relationship. In other words, a pretty girl is nice, but they need to learn to look for attributes of more substance. That said, there are at least five substantive questions you can train your kids to ask as they consider the guys and girls around them.

1. How does he or she treat others?

Perhaps the easiest way to quickly evaluate a person's character is to examine how they treat others, especially in those moments when they think nobody is looking. It might be wise to encourage your children to memorize the fruit of the Spirit found in Galatians 5:22-23, and then use this list as a quick mental checklist of things to look for in the people around them. Nobody is perfect, but someone who more often than not naturally displays *"love, joy, peace, patience, kindness, goodness, faithfulness, gentleness, and self-control"* as they interact with others is probably the type of person you want your kids to notice.

2. Does he or she operate with humility?

In our media-driven world (where whoever has the most friends or followers wins), it has become increasingly normal for young people to work extra hard to draw attention to themselves. Because everything seems to be a competition today, young people are constantly comparing themselves to their peers. This can very easily develop into an inner attitude of conceit that suggests they are better than others. The apostle Paul commands in Philippians 2:3 that we should *"do nothing out of selfish ambition or vain conceit. Rather, in humility value others above yourselves."* Because humility is a basic trait of the transformed life (and a rarity in this culture), you can train your kids to look for it in others.

3. How does he or she spend free time?

Young people today are busier than ever, but they still have some measure of free time to do as they please. How they spend this time reflects a great deal on what is important to them. Consider the truth found in Ephesians 5: 15-16: *"Be very careful, then, how you live—not as unwise but as wise, making the most of every opportunity, because the days are evil."* Young people can learn a lot about their peers by taking note of how they spend their free time. Does a boy waste a lot of time on TV or video games? He might be lazy. Does a girl spend way too much time on personal hygiene? She might be too into her looks. Does a boy spend all his time taking care of his car? He will probably care about it more than he cares about her. Ultimately, you want to lead your kids to notice if their peers spend a portion of their time focusing on things that have eternal value: specifically by developing their character and by investing in the lives of others. Kids that do this will typically stand out from the crowd.

4. How does he or she respond to authority?

A fairly consistent indicator of maturity in a young adult can be seen in how he or she relates to authority figures. While adolescents may be hard-wired to question authority, a potential boyfriend who has a pattern of rebellion should be a clear warning sign for your daughters to stay away. Paul makes it clear in Romans 3:2 that *"whoever rebels against the authority is rebelling against what God has instituted, and those who do so will bring judgment on themselves."* The key here is to examine attitudes, not just behaviors. You should train your kids to see the significance of how their peers respond to the authority of parents, teachers, and other adults in their lives. Specifically, you can teach your kids that the way a person submits to authority reveals a great deal about how they will honor God and honor their spouse in a long-term relationship.

5. Does he or she speak naturally about Christ?

It is very tempting to evaluate a person's faith by how involved she is in church activities. However, my experience is that church attendance is not always a reliable litmus test for Christian maturity. A better way to evaluate the substance of a person's faith is to observe how easily and comfortably she speaks about Christ in her life. A regenerate young person who is allowing God to transform her life will speak of Him naturally. Hebrews 13:15 captures this well: *"Through Jesus, therefore, let us continually offer to God a sacrifice of praise—the fruit of lips that openly profess his name."* If a person truly has an authentic faith, words describing Christ's activity will naturally come out of her mouth as a part of her daily life.

As we train our children and teenagers to examine these character traits that they begin to notice in the opposite-sex, the big message we want to communicate is that the opposite-sex is pretty cool. When my daughter notices a good-looking and charming guy, I should celebrate it with her. When my son starts paying attention to an attractive girl, I should celebrate with him. I should teach them that it is very likely in God's plan that they will one day marry. Thus, it is worthwhile to start exploring and observing what it is they are looking for in a spouse.

While the questions above can serve as a great filter for our kids to examine others, these things can also serve as a guide as they look in the mirror. In addition to looking for the right person, we should invest time and energy into training them to *become* the right person. This is probably the most important "preparation" lesson we can teach them.

nine

Modesty

Ladies, It's Not About You

For the last five or ten years, "hot" has become the operative word to describe good looks in our culture. Magazines release their lists of the hottest celebrities. Entire websites are devoted to helping people to determine how "hot" they are. I will often see my married guy friends playfully posting on Twitter that "My wife is hot." This simple three-letter word has become both a compliment and an essential descriptor of a person's attractiveness in our world.

Jenifer doesn't particularly like the word. This is a truth I learned when I posted something to the effect of "I have a hot wife" on Facebook a few years back. It made her uncomfortable. Her problem was that "hot" tends to imply sexiness, skin, and outward beauty, and nothing else. While she certainly likes that I am still very attracted to her physically, Jenifer wants to be seen as so much more than that. Words like beautiful, lovely, or captivating seem to work better, but we probably don't hear our kids saying those words too often. Instead, we will most likely hear "hot."

This is the dilemma with our world's definition of beauty. It focuses almost exclusively on the value of good looks and sexiness but gives little mention of a person's character. While our culture seems to suggest that being hot is of vital importance, we can see that it ultimately doesn't deliver what it promises. We can see this every time a supermodel's marriage implodes because of infidelity. Guys around the world think to themselves: "If I were married to her, I would never consider looking at another woman." But they are wrong. Even the Scripture reminds us that *"beauty is vain."* Being well-endowed with hotness is not enough to sustain a relationship.

I like the movie *Shallow Hal* for that reason. Jack Black plays a superficial man who only notices and values the sexy dimension of the women in his life. While stuck in an elevator, a self-help guru hypnotizes him and enables him to only see inner beauty. From that point onward, we see the world through his eyes. Obviously, his love interest is an overweight woman with a very good heart. What is most interesting to me is how the movie portrays the outwardly sexy women in his life. Suddenly, they are wrinkled, worn, and downright repulsive. I imagine that this is what ultimately happens when a man marries a supermodel who is the poster child for sex appeal but who is lacking in character. The more time he spends with her, the less attractive she becomes.

If we believe that our over-sexualized culture is a monster, then we have to consider the possibility that dressing with the goal of looking sexy serves as a means to "feed the beast." (To be clear, I am not suggesting that women should downplay their feminine beauty. Not at all. Their beauty is a reflection of our Creator and should be celebrated. However, there is a big difference between celebrating beauty and deliberately striving to be noticed as "hot.") There are at least three significant impacts of this issue on a girl's life.

1. Emphasizing "Hot" Impacts Their View of Self

We cannot deny that we live in a world that places a very high value on "hot." We celebrate the best looks, the skinniest body, and the shapeliest figure. Our girls are being raised in an environment that tells them that their looks are what matters most. Because of this, our girls are tempted and pressured to look the part and play up their "sexiness." If we are not careful, they will grow up believing that it is a vital necessity to look "hot." They will evaluate their value as a person based on whether or not they measure up to a completely unrealistic standard.

While there is nothing wrong with a girl striving to accentuate her feminine beauty, it becomes a problem when she emphasizes her outsides over her inner character. I remind brides of this at weddings when I read from I Peter 3:3-4. Peter reminds women of something that parents should regularly remind their daughters: *"Your beauty should not come from outward adornment, such as braided hair and the wearing of gold jewelry and fine clothes. Instead, it should be that of your inner self, the unfading beauty of a gentle and quiet spirit, which is of great worth in God's sight."* There is so much more to beauty than what is on the outside.

2. Emphasizing "Hot" Impacts How Men See Them

Guys are visual, having a God-given propensity to fixate on sexual beauty. This awareness of girls and their sexual attractiveness is what draws a man to a mate and keeps him coming back to her. However, this tendency has a dark side. What God designed to powerfully attract Adam to Eve unfortunately makes Adam keenly aware of all the other Eves around him. For most, this tempts men to look at other women, often to the point of entertaining lustful thoughts. In some cases, it can even lead to foolish decisions that result in significant sexual sins.

While young men are universally aware of this struggle, young women are typically divided into three different camps regarding their knowledge of it and the part that modesty plays. One group knows that men are visual and they play into it, dressing as sexy as possible. A larger group is entirely oblivious, dressing however they want, thinking it doesn't matter. A third group is aware of how men think and therefore dress in a way that strives to honor and protect those around them.

We typically notice the girls in group number one from a mile away. They like boys to notice them so they dress in ways that intentionally draw their attention. Sadly, girls who put their bodies and their sexuality on display like this may get awareness from boys in the short term, but they are the same ones who the boys become bored with and discard like a consumable.

82

The second group is probably the biggest. My experience is that most teenage girls are oblivious to the struggle that the young men around them are experiencing. They simply don't understand it. This leads them to the wrong conclusion that showing a little skin or striving to look "sexy" (which in many ways has become synonymous with "stylish") is no big deal. Any man on the planet will admit that it is, in fact, a very big deal.

A third group of girls dresses with more wisdom than the other two. They do not suppress or ignore their feminine beauty, but they strive to present it with a healthy dose of modesty. They understand how the men in their lives are tempted to fixate on the female body. These girls realize that while this is not their fault, they may be required to adjust their lives accordingly. If not, they run the risk of being noticed and remembered on only one dimension.

3. Emphasizing "Hot" Impacts How They Reflect God

Ephesians 5:3 gives a basic target for believers to aim for: *"But among you there must not be even a hint of sexual immorality, or of any kind of impurity, or of greed, because these are improper for God's holy people."* While this passage doesn't talk specifically about clothes, many of the styles that are common in women's fashion work against this basic command. Even if the wearer is naïve and has no thoughts of sexuality, their actions can potentially lead men to immediately think of nothing but.

While it is easy to write off Paul's directive as oppressive and legalistic, I don't think his point is to suppress the liberties of the individual believer. Instead, it is as if Paul is saying, "Don't outwardly flaunt your sexuality, because it's not who you are." Or even better: "It doesn't reflect *Whose* you are." If we are called to be holy by God and enabled to be holy by the cross, then this inner holiness should be evident when people look at us. Granted, Jesus had much to say to the Pharisees who looked good on the outside but had corrupt hearts on the inside. Reflecting God's character must always start deep inside our hearts and lives. It should also be evident on the impressions that we make on people.

The topic of modesty and what it means to each individual girl and how she presents herself is not going away. It will probably create tension and conflict every time a mother and daughter go shopping for clothes. It will show up every time girls are gathered at the neighborhood pool. That is why we need to start early on getting our daughters thinking about these issues.

Several years ago a report on CNN caught my attention. The talking head on the screen was describing a recent study of young girls and their tendency to grow up too quickly in our culture. A credible team at a prominent university conducted the research and the American Psychological Association was releasing the report, so it was getting some significant press. Their findings? The early sexualization of girls is a bad thing. CNN spent a good part of an hour on the report, complete with authors, Ph.D.s and child psychologists, who all furrowed their brows in a scholarly fashion and announced that this was "disturbing" news. They specifically focused upon the media influence of sexy young female music artists (who have a devout following among many pre-teens) and their success in normalizing a form of sexuality among those in their audience.

Our girls will feel the impact of our culture early on and it will powerfully influence what they define as fashionable. Their peers will impact them, too, but their peers are mainly getting their ideas from the larger culture in which they live. To be honest, we never know where that is going to go next.

Parents must begin thinking about the issues of dress and modesty when their girls are very young, long before there is even a hint of sexuality in them. If not, they are setting themselves up for a significant battle when their girls make the transition into adolescence. Let me explain that statement.

I'm not a big fan of bikinis. I regularly take heat from others on this issue, but it only makes me dig in my heels deeper. I wouldn't dream of letting my daughters leave the house in their underwear, so why would I allow them to hang out at a pool party with their friends wearing the swimwear equivalent? I don't. However, the need to address that with my girls started long before they were teenagers.

Let's say a string bikini looks cute on my three-year-old. It looks cute when she is five. It still does at eight and ten. This becomes her normal swimwear. Every summer she gets a new bikini. Then one year in her early teens she gets something else: curves. Suddenly, what was cute on a little girl's frame screams something entirely different. As a parent who is dedicated to helping my daughter to not be seen as a sex object by her guy friends, I decide that her bikini days are over. So I tell her.

How do I picture that conversation working out for me?

What was perfectly fine and normal for ten years is suddenly not allowed? Would any sane person picture my daughter saying, "Thanks, Dad. That's completely reasonable." Probably not. Here's a lesson worth heeding: I can't easily change my entire family's bathing suit policy the summer my daughter develops a body. That's why it is best to start establishing some guidelines for modesty far sooner than you think.

How to Talk About Modesty

With Younger Girls

I have a six-year-old in my house right now and, left to her own devices, she would have no problem running through the house naked on a daily basis. We have had to instruct her that she cannot do that. Similarly, from her early preschool years, you can begin to teach your daughter that her private parts need to be protected. You can simply explain that the parts of her body that are covered by a bathing suit are special and that they belong to her alone. Nobody should touch her there and she should be careful to cover herself. Obviously, you can explain that mom and dad or siblings might help give her a bath or get her dressed, but that the general rule should be to guard her body. This lays a simple foundation that can be built on as she gets older.

With Older Girls

As a girl enters the tween years, she begins to search for her own identity. With all that she sees around her, your daughter needs the reassurance that she is beautiful and significant. She particularly needs to hear this from her father. It is at this stage that you should affirm all the positive traits you see in her, especially the inner qualities of her heart and character. You can also begin to teach her that girls who flaunt their bodies usually make a powerful first impression on boys. The bad news is that it is likely all the boys will remember. A good question to pose to your daughter is: "As you grow up, do you want to be primarily known for your body when there is so much more to who you are?" Then you must be sure to affirm all the other amazing things you see in her. After all, she won't know unless you tell her. The assurance that she is precious both inside and out will go a long way to giving her the self-worth that will sustain her through the turbulent teen years, if only just barely.

With Teenage Girls

Adolescent girls should be regularly reminded that when a man sees a woman's skin (or her cleavage or a glimpse of her underwear or anything else that is sexual in nature), his mind has a hard time focusing on anything else. In his book, *The Complete Guide to Guys*, Dave Barry describes an experience of walking on the beach with some friends when they encountered a topless woman sunbathing out of the corners of their eyes. He summarized their brain activity as follows: "Portion of brainpower dedicated to conversation, thinking about world events, maintaining bodily activities such as respiration: 5%. Portion of brainpower devoted to taking a gander at sunbathing woman's breasts: 95%."[1] We are ashamed to say it, but most men can relate to this description.

While I want my lovely teenage daughter with her cute little figure to fully grasp the need to not be a stumbling block to her Christian brothers, she may not listen to me. That is understandable. After all, I'm an out-of-touch dinosaur. It is likely that the only way my daughter is going to grasp a teenage guy's perspective is for her to hear it directly from a teen guy. I cannot recommend highly enough the book *For Young Women Only* by Shaunti Feldhahn. Chapter five is required reading for each of my daughters. What they will find there are actual quotes from numerous guys as they describe what is going on in their heads when a girl shows even a little bit of skin. It is absolutely eye opening. Make your teen daughter read it!

No matter how old your daughters are, you can always look for opportunities to use the stories of Scripture to illustrate the fundamental principles of human behavior. After all, there is truly nothing new under the sun. The story of David and Bathsheba in 2 Samuel 11 captures how guys can so easily be tempted visually. Verse 2 characterizes our common struggle: *"One evening David got up from his bed and walked around on the roof of the palace. From the roof he saw a woman bathing. The woman was very beautiful."* David, a man after God's own heart, found himself tempted by a sexually-charged situation. We know where that led him: adultery, murder, and a number of other undesirable things.

While our girls might not ever fully grasp this struggle within a man's brain, heart, and eyes, they must be consistently taught that it does exist. Sadly, while this immature tendency toward sin is not the female gender's fault, in many ways it is their problem. That is why parents must deliberately teach the values of modest behavior and dress to their daughters. Because the struggle found in their Christian brothers is not going away.

ten

Chivalry

Training Our Sons to Honor and Protect Women

Over the past five or six years, the *Twilight* books and movies have been a pretty big deal with teenage girls. Beyond the brooding yet good-looking vampires and the hunky (and often shirtless) werewolves, I have been trying to figure out why these movies have been so successful. Actually, from the "oohs" and "ahhs" I hear from my daughters' friends, the "beefcake factor" may be enough. I would have loved to have heard a girl be completely honest and declare at the ticket window: "I'd like two tickets to the seven o'clock showing of Taylor Lautner's abs, please." Nevertheless, I've got to think something bigger is going on here.

A few years ago, Jenifer and I were in a ladies' clothing store and I noticed a *Twilight* book sitting behind the checkout counter. While Jen tried a few things on, I struck up a conversation with the young woman who owned the book. She told me she was on her third reading of the series. I asked point-blank: "What's the big deal? Why do you like these books so much?"

Her response was eye opening. She shared with me that the books describe a wonderful, yet impossible scenario: a romantic, too-good-to-be-true gentleman whose pursuit of the woman leaves her feeling cherished and not used. She summarized it this way: "Edward goes to incredible lengths to protect Bella, even from himself. He loves her so much that he will sacrifice everything to take care of her." As she said these words, her eyes expressed the sad reality that she had come to embrace in her own life: it's not real. Guys aren't like that anymore.

Perhaps she was right.

In her mind—and in the minds of most young women—men always want something. Unfortunately, in our over-sexed culture, that usually means some form of "putting out." To get (or keep) the guy, the girl is tempted to give him what he wants. Sadly, these young women fail to realize that when they give sex away before marriage, they are removing the primary motivator the man needs to commit. After all, why should he pursue her when she's giving him what he desires most? The result is ultimately women who lose out in a culture full of men who are takers. Apparently, the guys from *Twilight* are just the opposite of that.

As the store clerk and I talked, she shared that she was currently living with her boyfriend and that, while he was a good guy, she yearned for something more. Something like what she saw on display in the *Twilight* books. I insisted to her that there were still guys who think like that out there. But I don't think she believed me. Apparently, I've officially entered my "clueless old guy" life-stage.

How many girls like her are settling for second best in their relationships, all because there are so few young men whose parents have instilled in them the importance of chivalrous behavior and practice?

My experience is that most young men tend to be users of women, not protectors. Many will grow out of it as they get older and learn to think more of others than themselves, but their teenage drives are particularly prone to self-centered behaviors and tendencies. Our culture has allowed it and overly aggressive girls have permitted, even encouraged it. It's not the girls' fault, but in many cases their desire to be loved and wanted has caused them to lower the bar on their expectation of chivalry and sacrifice from the men in their lives. Our young women have allowed our young men to get away with it.

I would suggest that the typical teenage boy doesn't spend a lot of time thinking about how to guard, protect, and care for the girls he encounters. There are the rare few who have been taught otherwise by their fathers, but most haven't given it much thought. These young men probably do not have evil intentions, but if they have not been intentionally taught and equipped to have a chivalrous mindset, they are likely to end up inadvertently taking advantage of girls instead of honoring them. They might find themselves acting in stark contrast to the medieval knights who were first characterized by the word chivalry.

These are the boys that our sons are likely to interact with in school, on the ball fields and in the locker room. If they do not know a different, better way of interacting with and caring for girls and women, they are likely to act and think just like their peers. Therefore, we want to train our boys from the earliest possible age to have a "sixth sense" that enables them to tell that something isn't right about how other guys treat the girls in their lives. The earlier we start, the earlier it will be ingrained into who they are.

Boys must be taught from an early age that there is a certain calling upon men to protect and care for women. Starting with their mother and their sisters, boys should be coached in some of the basic disciplines of chivalry. As they begin to build these habits into their home lives, they will come to apply these behaviors and attitudes to all the women they encounter.

How to Talk About Chivalry

In a perfect world, a father should take responsibility for training his son to be chivalrous: to make honoring and protecting women a natural part of who he is. A father can both teach what it looks like and model these attitudes and behaviors as he cares for his wife in the home. The single mom who lacks a strong father figure for her son can teach chivalry, as well. She can effectively leverage the heart relationship between mother and son to raise the bar high for how he should treat her and the other women in his life.

To get chivalry into the conversation of your home, you can begin with the broad concept that men are called to take care of women. Point out that men are typically bigger and stronger than women, so God expects men to use their strength for good things and not for bad things: things as simple as letting girls go first, opening their doors, carrying heavy things, and standing in front of them if there is danger.

As your son gets older, you can begin to elaborate the general concept of chivalry into more abstract values that apply to his mom and sisters but also to every other woman in his life. Four values that should be championed are protection, honor, gentleness, and sacrifice. Sooner than later, you would be wise to specifically connect those four values to how your sons treat any girl they are interested in romantically.

1. Providing Protection

Our young men must understand that when a girl is with them, they are taking responsibility for her protection and well-being. They are temporarily taking on the role that was given by God to the girl's father. In extreme cases, this might require an extraordinary level of bravery and courage from them. However, this issue of protection shows up in everyday situations, as well. It has implications to how our sons drive, where they take their dates, and how they protect the young women in their lives from what is perhaps the most surprising of threats: themselves. This is one thing the *Twilight* movies got right.

A chivalrous young man who is beginning to dip his toes into a romantic relationship will realize that the potential for becoming sexually intimate is a real possibility. He will make sure that he avoids situations that might lead to temptation for either him or the girl. He will be aware of how easy it is to cross moral boundaries in their relationship so he will be diligent to protect the relationship and, just as important, the reputation of the girl. Furthermore, there is a need for emotional protection, too.

Because girls can have an overly romanticized view of how boy/girl relationships should go, they are often prone to quickly getting their hearts tied up in an emotional dependence that the guy is oblivious of. He thinks it's a good friendship or a casual dating relationship while she is at home dreaming about what it would be like to be married to him. Men are not typically known for this kind of deep introspection about their relationships. Women are. They begin to hone these skills at an early age, so you must be diligent to talk with your sons about how easily a girl's heart can be caught up in an emotional relationship.

Another thing you can tell your boys is to not be careless with the words "I love you." A young woman who might be coming from an emotionally needy or broken place can put far more weight into those words than a young man ever means. I once heard a wise man say: "Don't say 'I love you' unless the next words out of your mouth will be 'Will you marry me?'" Not bad advice.

2. Giving Honor

Every woman desires to be treasured and put upon a pedestal of honor. Ideally, this need will be met by a girl's father and she will expect nothing short of that from the other men in her life. Unfortunately, the fractured relationship between many fathers and daughters often causes girls to settle for far less than honor from men. While these girls may not demand honor and respect, our young men should give it nonetheless. Because that is what chivalrous men do.

One good rule of thumb is to train a boy to honor a girl exactly how he would if her father was standing right beside her. That will dictate how he speaks to her, treats her, and cares for her.

A final way we can teach our sons to display honor is to encourage them to affirm a girl's character far more than her physical attractiveness. Feminine beauty is a very good thing, something that God wired men to notice. However, when a guy affirms only a girl's beauty, she might begin to believe that's all she is. One way he honors the girl is by noticing and building up her heart and character. This will also serve as a means to equip him to begin to notice and appreciate those things in the girls in his life.

3. Demonstrating Gentleness

Gentleness is not often a characteristic used to describe pre-teen and teenage boys. Just go to a fast-food restaurant on a Saturday afternoon and compare a soccer team of boys with a soccer team of girls. While they are both having the same post-game celebration, their behaviors are markedly different. The girls are quietly talking and politely sharing napkins while the boys are loudly talking over one another, pushing each other around, and having burping contests. Typical boy behavior is the exact polar opposite of what I see from the gentlemen on *Downton Abbey*. (Yes, I'm into that show. Cut me some slack.)

While our boys need to be taught basic manners and common courtesy, gentleness implies far more than just an absence of rudeness. As they interact with the girls in their lives, boys must come to an early understanding of how husbands are called to treat their wives: as "weaker vessels" (see 1 Peter 3:7). As a married man of more than 23 years, I am still learning that my wife requires gentleness in how I care for her, talk to her, and even argue with her. I cannot interact with her in the same way that I do a guy friend.

Training in gentleness does not mean that we are encouraging our sons to go soft or even to "get in touch with their feminine side." In fact, it is just the opposite. True gentlemen are able to successfully channel their manhood in a way that is marked by both strength and tenderness; by an understanding that the feminine nature of women demands that we treat them differently. Our boys will not know how to operate with gentleness unless they are regularly reminded that it is an essential part of manhood.

4. Modeling Sacrifice

Finally, our sons must be trained to love like Jesus loved: generous, elaborate, and marked by sacrifice. Ephesians 5:25 commands husbands to be like Christ in this way: *"Husbands, love your wives, just as Christ loved the church and gave himself up for her."* Sacrificing self in order to meet the needs of another person is not a natural tendency for most men. Putting a ring on these guys' fingers and then expecting them to suddenly be able to love and live sacrificially is unrealistic. So if this counter-intuitive calling toward selflessness is the expectation for Christian husbands, then the expectation of a life marked by sacrifice should begin long before the guy walks the aisle.

Young boys with a self-centered bent should be consistently reminded of the need to put others first and to model Christ's sacrificial nature in every day things. When most men consider the Biblical call to *"lay down your life,"* they imagine throwing themselves in front of a bullet to save their wives. That's well and good, but the opportunity for a life and death sacrifice is probably not going to happen to most guys. Paul was advocating for sacrifice in the day-to-day things of life. Our boys need to learn that early.

> *Jenifer's Perspective:*
> *"While most men are willing to lay down their lives,*
> *what most women want is a man who will lay down the*
> *remote control to spend meaningful time with her."*

Likewise, there will be opportunities to teach your teenage sons what it looks like to demonstrate sacrifice in and through the dating relationships they enter. The most important lesson might be that they not be permitted to enter a dating relationship in the first place until they can prove that they can love sacrificially in the midst of it. While I experienced several long-term relationships in high school and college, I can recognize now that I didn't learn what selfless love was until I grew up a bit and arrived at marriage. Allowing our boys to "practice" love that is self-centered at its core only serves to handicap them for a successful marriage down the road. Wise parents will closely observe the maturity of their sons to determine if they are learning to love others in a sacrificial way.

The best way for our sons to learn this self-denying, Christ-like love is by watching good men loving the women in their lives. This critical part of Christian manhood is most powerfully embraced by the next generation when it is regularly witnessed first-hand. This puts a heavy but reasonable burden on fathers to make sure they love their wives in a way that can be easily copied by their sons.

94

Likewise, dads of daughters are not off the hook. They must model this kind of sacrifice with their wives so that their girls will know what to expect and require from the men who will eventually pursue them. Little eyes are always watching.

The Payoff of a Chivalrous Life

I can remember about fifteen years ago when the Promise Keepers movement was in full swing. Hundreds of thousands of men were gathering in football stadiums across America for worship and teaching. The general theme of the movement was to challenge men to Biblical manhood, devoted spiritual lives, and Christ-like leadership in their homes. Promise Keepers got some significant secular media attention and it was always interesting to hear the pundits weighing in on whether it was a good thing or not.

In the middle of all that, I stumbled upon an episode of *The View* where the women were discussing Promise Keepers. Three of the four women spoke harshly about it, insisting that it was a move backwards to a culture where wives had to follow the leadership of their husbands. It was apparent that the thought of men gathering together in these events and talking about Christian manhood made them furious. Then Star Jones, who had been quietly listening to the debate up to this point, spoke up for the first time. I will never forget what she said. With firm conviction in her voice, she said: "You give me a man who will love me like Jesus loves me, and I will follow him wherever he wants me to go." I haven't heard a better commentary on Ephesians 5 since.

What do young men get when their lives are marked by chivalry? When they make laying down their lives to love and protect the women in their lives a priority? When they learn to offer sacrificial and selfless love to their wives? Eventually, they get the honor, respect and commitment of the woman of their dreams. It may take a while to get there, but the payoff is so very worth it.

We must indoctrinate our sons with this irrefutable truth: the guy with the six-pack abs may make the girl say "oooh" and "ahhh," but she will eventually grow weary of him. It will be the righteous and selfless young man who will get the girl in the end, even if he is a bit of a geek. I know this from personal experience.

eleven

Selfishness

Why Typical Teen Dating is Poor Preparation for Marriage

In my role as family minister at a large church, I end up doing pastoral counseling with more than a few couples in marital crisis. They come to my office at varying levels of hurt and bitterness, looking for some relief from the pain that they are experiencing at home. While they are not prone to easily admit it, most of these struggling marriages share a common theme: selfishness. Sure, we talk about the pain from the past and the hurt feelings of today, but when all the layers are peeled back, the biggest obstacle to reconciliation and healing is a prevalence of self-centered thinking.

Until God begins to work on the hearts of the couples I counsel, my pointing out of self-centered behavior usually falls on deaf ears. Most are quick to note the faults of their spouse while justifying their own shortcomings. "Yeah, but he..." is a phrase I hear a lot more than "You're right, I..." Selfishness is like a cancer in marriage, slowly destroying things from the inside out.

At the core of each of our souls we find our sinful nature and our selfish heart holding hands and singing "Kumbaya." It is the part of us that says, "I want my way" and asks, "What is in it for me?" While

97

we are all prone to selfishness, this capacity must be slowly put to death if a marriage is to thrive.

Selfish thinking is at the foundation of the unbiblical belief that God wants you to be happy at all costs. If your spouse fails to read your mind and to meet your every need, you begin to consider the possibility that you married the wrong one. The popular idea that your spouse should "complete you" has led to people seeking a "soul mate" instead of a committed relationship. It has resulted in a multi-million dollar online dating industry that promises to find you the perfectly compatible match. While compatibility is certainly worthwhile, we cannot presume that finding "the one" will free us from the responsibility of hard work and commitment in marriage.

If a dysfunctional marriage is the major league of relational selfishness, then dating is the bush league. It is the training ground where young people can learn the four-step cycle of flirt/date/break up/repeat. This generally accepted cycle of most dating relationships is fueled almost exclusively by selfishness. When one person doesn't live up to the other's (poorly defined) expectations and fails to meet their needs, the relationship becomes unworkable. One of the two loses interest or unsatisfied with the relationship and ends it. Typically, someone moves on and someone has a broken heart. Both are left with baggage.

What leads to a typical break-up? What is going on in the mind of the one who is dissatisfied? There are certainly exceptions, but it is usually rooted in selfishness: the other person didn't meet MY needs. She didn't make ME happy. If I feel this way, my only choice is to discard her and look for a person who can successfully meet all my wants and needs.

This habit can certainly be carried into marriage, but even our culture is shifting, providing a buffer zone before making a lifelong commitment. It is called cohabitation. Instead of expecting people to give up their selfishness and truly commit to laying down their lives for one another, living together provides a time-extension on selfish thinking.

Cohabitation has increased in the United States by more than 1,500% over the past 50 years. The number of couples living together in 1960 was about 450,000. Today, the number is more than 7.5 million. It has become so normative in our culture that the majority of marriages today will be preceded by a time of living together.[1] In a study conducted by the National Marriage Project, 66% of high school senior boys and 61% of senior girls indicated that they agreed with the statement "it is usually a good idea for a couple to live together before getting married in order to find out whether they really get along."[2]

If you want to try something interesting, read your teenager the quote from the study above and see if they agree or disagree with it. Get them to tell you why they believe what they believe. It might make for an eye-opening discussion of how they arrived at their conclusions.

The next generation is focusing more and more on the nebulous goal of compatibility and rejecting the value of commitment and fidelity. They can even spiritualize it by believing that "God has created the perfect person out there just for me." While God is sovereign and surely knows who we will marry, this thinking is fraught with all sorts of problems, most notably that it wrongly allows our kids to put more effort into finding the right person than on becoming the right person. Our culture of serial dating and cohabitation certainly doesn't help.

> *Jenifer's Perspective:*
> *"I have had many young women over the years try to convince me that they married 'the wrong one.' What they don't know is that if they trade him in, the next guy will be the wrong one, too. There is no such thing as 'the one' as every marriage is challenging."*

Typical dating habits teach kids how to be really good at breaking up. Training kids in serial dating can easily lead to serial marriage, where one can cast aside their spouse when they no longer meet their needs. It scares the heck out of me.

The natural bent of every young child is selfishness. Babies want what they want when they want it. They do not have any concern for the needs and desires of others. As they grow and develop, they gradually learn some type of empathy. Some get this and some do not. As abstract thought becomes more and more prevalent in the early teen years, they will become more able to consider the perspective of others and hopefully become less selfish.

The development of this type of empathy is a slow process, but one that must be nurtured by parents who consistently encourage their children to lay aside their selfish motives to consider the needs of others. Obviously, this is a foundational part of training our kids that starts when they are toddlers and continues into young adulthood.

As we encourage unselfish thinking in our children, one application that should be consistently on our minds is their eventual romantic relationships. One goal would be that our kids not approach potential dating relationships with a "what's in it for me?" attitude. In fact, we can even tell them that as they are getting older: "You will not be free to enter a dating relationship until you give clear evidence of selflessness at home." They won't be perfect, of course, but it can be a goal to aim for.

How to Talk About Selfishness

The day will eventually come when your teenagers want to be in a dating relationship. They probably don't have impure motives; they are just following their hearts. No matter their age, it is unlikely that they will be in touch enough with their feelings to recognize the hints of selfishness within themselves. One way to help your teens to process through this is to ask a few simple questions: "Why do you want to be with _____? Why do you want to go out with her?"

Asking questions, getting answers, and then asking more questions might help our teenager to see that their interest in the other person is, at its foundation, selfishly motivated. If you can get past their initial grunts and their looks that seem to say, "You are a weirdo parent," both you and your teen might learn something. If they are honest, they will eventually realize that they are interested in the other person for a couple of key reasons:

- They make me feel good.
- There is security in knowing that someone is interested in me.

- There is pride/honor in being able to declare that he/she is mine.
- I want to be loved. He/she is a person of value who has declared that I am valuable.

These are common desires in every person, but they are not necessarily healthy. Just because we all desire these things, it does not mean that we should affirm or encourage them. Furthermore, we shouldn't encourage our kids to enter relationships based upon these typical reasons.

When we peel back the layers of selfish thinking, we ultimately realize that our culture's widely accepted definition of "love" is actually rooted in self-centeredness. When the average young person says, "I love you," what they are essentially saying is, "I love how you make me feel." At the core of that love is actually a love of self. "I love you because of what you do for me." Allowing our kids to practice that kind of "love" does nothing to prepare them for a Christ-like, sacrificial love that endures when feelings wane and circumstances are difficult.

Instead, we should be diligent to train our kids in the opposite of selfishness. By example and instruction, we must teach them to love as Jesus loved. As they give evidence of unconditional, selfless love with those who are closest to them, the time will eventually come when we feel they can enter into a healthy relationship with someone else. It will take tremendous wisdom to know when the time is right, but God wants to lead us in this.

Is Significance the Real Problem?

Beyond their self-centered motives, most of the reasons that young people give for wanting a boyfriend/girlfriend are rooted in a desire for significance and worth. Could it be that the main reason our Christian kids are searching for a relationship with the opposite-sex is that they have tried Jesus and found him to be wholly unfulfilling?

Years ago I heard youth communicator Neil McClendon say, "The faith of the average 17-year-old is sort of like his 5th grade science fair project. Mom and dad did all the work and he just put his name on it." I think he's right. Most of the kids raised in our "good Christian homes" have not truly experienced a meaningful relationship with Christ where they can *"taste and see that the Lord is good."*

Much of this might be due to the push in our evangelical churches for our kids to get saved at 6 or 7 years old, where children can articulate a profession of faith in Christ but do not have the abstract, experiential encounter with Christ that rocks them to the core. With these kids, parents have a sense of accomplishment that their child has been baptized (and is thus secure in the faith) but then they move on to other goals: good grades, athletic achievement, popularity, etc. They don't consider what it looks like for their kids to be grounded in the faith, to grow in Godliness, to learn to experience God every day.

Thus, many of our kids never fall in love with their Savior and find him to be altogether satisfying. They have an intense longing to connect, to be needed, to be loved...all longings that only God can satisfy. Unfortunately, they bypass their Creator (God) and look to the created (another teenager) to get their deepest needs met.

These young people eventually stand at an altar, making their vows, pledging their all and their lives and their futures to each other. But what they are really saying is this: "I'm counting on you to 'complete me.' I'm depending on you to give me my identity and meaning in life. I'm counting on you to meet my every need."

They probably don't say it quite like that (though more and more modern weddings with personally written vows are using that sort of language), but it is going through their minds. Why? Because they have been looking for that in other people all their young lives...and they think they have finally found it.

I can assure you with almost 100% certainty that their spouse will eventually be a disappointment. Why? Because they are expecting their spouse to be something that only God can be.

Parents must teach their children that their worth and purpose and identity can never be found in another person. It can only be found in the person of Jesus Christ. Our kids need to be regularly reminded that they are who they are because of who their Creator says they are. They need to be taught that they are completely valued by a God who loves unconditionally. They must be indoctrinated with the truth that no human relationship can satisfy them like a relationship with Jesus can.

At the core of giving our kids a healthy perspective of sex and boy/girl relationships is teaching them to connect with Christ in a meaningful and truly satisfying way. Unfortunately, many Christian parents can't make a convincing argument for this because they have never found God to be all that satisfying in their own lives.

In a high school Psychology class that I teach each week at our church's private school, the students and I were discussing this issue as it relates to high divorce rates, even within the church. Lauren, a bright senior, wisely pointed out: "How can we expect people to find lasting satisfaction and stay committed in a relationship with a fallen, imperfect person when most people have been unable to find that with a holy, perfect God?" Her point was not that God is unsatisfying, but that most people don't first find their identity in Christ before they invest in a romantic relationship.

Sadly, this is true for many adult Christians. It is certainly true for most teenagers. May we learn to deal with selfish thinking in our lives at the root of the problem: our need to be loved completely by the only One who can truly satisfy. May we allow Him to transform our hearts and the hearts of our kids so powerfully that they enter relationships not looking for what they can get from them, but for what they can give.

twelve

Reality

The Awful Truth About Boyfriends and Girlfriends

When it comes to celebrity watching, our culture has what I would consider to be an unhealthy obsession with knowing who is in a relationship with whom. We read our tabloids and watch *TMZ*, all the while hoping and wondering: "Are they more than just friends? Will this be true love? Will the relationship last? When will they finally get married?" As consumers of entertainment, we have become almost as interested in the personal and relational lives of artists as we are in the art they create.

Case in point: Taylor Swift.

The public has been absolutely mesmerized by her dating life ever since she entered the spotlight. If there is even a morsel of truth in the tabloids, I'm beginning to think that Swift can't handle the possibility of being without a significant other.

When she was nineteen it was Joe Jonas. Then she dated the much younger Taylor Lautner. There was John Mayer for a while. Rumor has it that there was a brief stint with Eddie Redmayne. She made the cover of *Us* magazine with beau Jake Gyllenhaal. Then she made headlines when she dated American royalty in the form of

Conor Kennedy. Next it was Harry Styles of One Direction. She might have had a relationship with British singer Ed Sheeran. I even read that she is interested in meeting Prince Harry. By the time you read these words, she may have gotten married or foregone relationships altogether. (But then what would she write songs about?)

While we can try to downplay Swift's apparent need to constantly have a boyfriend, we cannot deny the fact that young stars like her serve to both reflect and influence the culture as a whole. As a parent whose kids are constantly digesting media in myriad forms, this troubles me. I am concerned that we are raising a generation of kids who are evaluating their value and identity based upon their relationship status on Facebook. The net result is that even our youngest adolescents feel the pressure to have a boyfriend or girlfriend.

Because they see the glamor and romance of their favorite stars' relationships played out in full detail, our kids have the real potential to develop an unrealistic view of what having a boyfriend or girlfriend is really like. Our younger teens—who are emotionally immature yet who see their friends pairing up—are particularly prone to this.

These kids are in dire need for their parents to give them a dose of reality; to love them enough to tell them the truth about having a boyfriend or girlfriend. For once we pull back the curtain, there are a few undeniable truths about the typical teen romantic relationship.

A Relationship Will Ruin a Friendship

Few kids have the ability to think through the ways that relationships are likely to play out in the long term, especially regarding what it will do to their friendships.

When my oldest daughter Lindsey was in the 7th grade, she and Jenifer went on a mission trip with the students from our church. While the team of 100 teenagers was scattered into different groups and vans, Jenifer noticed that one boy in particular kept showing up to talk to Lindsey. Jake was handsome, charming, and popular. And he was obviously flirting with my daughter.

Late one night at bedtime, Lindsey sat down on Jenifer's bed and told her that Jake had asked her to "go out with him." Of course, they

105

had no plans to go anywhere, but that was the current term for being boyfriend/girlfriend. (Becoming "Facebook official" was still a faraway dream.) She was obviously excited, but she wanted her mom's thoughts on the whole thing.

Since this was our first time as parents to deal with this issue, Jenifer kept her composure and agreed that Jake was a great guy. It was the perfect opportunity to affirm Lindsey in that such a sharp young man had seen something special in her. Then she shifted gears. Jenifer tried to help Lindsey to think through the long-term realities of what would happen if she and Jake "went out together."

She asked if Lindsey enjoyed having Jake as a friend. Of course, she said yes. Then Jenifer told her how "going out" would eventually play out. Lindsey and Jake would see each other at church events or sit together in worship. They would maybe talk on the phone. They would do all the things that young couples do.

Then eventually one of them would grow tired of the other and they would break up. There would be some hurt feelings. Things from then on would be very awkward in that it would be difficult to be friends. Jenifer suggested to Lindsey that if she valued her friendship with Jake, it would be best if they didn't become boyfriend/girlfriend. Lindsey agreed and the two of them remained good friends for many years.

Most kids do not realize that it is hard to maintain a relationship once the romance ends. The old breakup line of "we can still be friends" has never worked out for anybody in the history of mankind.

A Relationship Will Be a Burden

A teenager will develop a crush on someone and begin to imagine what every day will be like once they are an "item." They picture their days being filled with an endless supply of affection, attention, and affirmation. What they fail to realize is that those very things can eventually smother their lives. When one person in the relationship is more needy than they other, then someone is going to start realizing that it's just not worth it.

We know a young man who found himself in a serious relationship in 9th grade. His busy life was already filled with schoolwork, baseball, and family activities. Now he also had a girl who he was obligated to spend time with and talk to regularly. Add texting to the mix and he found himself having to be constantly managing the relationship.

If he didn't check in with her about his plans each night or respond immediately to the seemingly endless bombardment of texts each day, she got upset, wondering what was wrong. "Do you still like me? What's wrong? Is there someone else?"

He eventually confessed to his parents that while he still liked the girl, he felt that having a girlfriend at this stage of life wasn't worth the emotional effort. In fact, the relationship had become something of a pain. He just wanted to be a kid for a little while longer; one who does schoolwork and plays baseball with his friends.

For our kids who are far removed from a stage of life when they are beginning to think about marriage, dating relationships can be a significant burden that has very little to offer in terms of an up-side. We need to make sure our kids are well prepared for the realities of the down-side. Most notably, the fact that:

A Relationship Will Be a Source of Sexual Temptation

While God invented sex and wants us to enjoy it, He gives clear direction that it is reserved for marriage. Yet our kids run headfirst into situations that set them up for overwhelming temptation. Any romantic relationship will, by its very nature, create powerful opportunities for unwise decisions regarding our sexuality. An engaged couple that is striving for holiness in the days leading up to their wedding day has a fighting chance. After all, the end is near. However, young couples who are nowhere near that stage of life are just asking for trouble.

That is why I love what Pastor Mark Driscoll says. He was once anonymously asked, "If I am too young for marriage is it wrong to date?" Driscoll answered with an emphatic, "Yes!" He went on to explain:

> Why would you take a gal out and get emotionally connected, maybe cross sexual lines knowing that this has no future?

107

Why? That's using someone. Because you are lonely. Because you like companionship. Because you like sexual favors. Honestly, if you are asking this question, would you date one of my daughters? Would you walk up to me and say, "I know I'm not ready to marry and I have no intentions to marry, but I'm just looking for someone to hang out with and get emotionally connected to and maybe have occasional sexual contact with. So could I have your daughter for a few years?" If you wouldn't do that to me as your pastor, then don't do it to anybody.[1]

Driscoll's view is pretty radical, but it's honest. Our kids need parents who will clearly communicate to them that any boyfriend/girlfriend relationship has the potential for sexual sin. While this might feel awkward, we have to get comfortable talking about it.

How to Talk About the Reality of Relationships

We all know the phrase "people-watch." I often do this at airports, trying to guess a family's backstory, using only their appearance for clues. If I am sitting near them and can hear them talk, I feel like my guesses are a lot more accurate. I imagine their whole life story: where they are from, what they do for a living, and what they are struggling with in life. Sure, it's shallow, but it's cheap entertainment when I am waiting on a flight.

One thing you can do to help your children to see the reality of teen relationships is to teach them to "couple-watch." Without being rude or intrusive, train them to watch the couples they know. Even elementary-aged kids can learn to examine teenagers at church or in the community and see how they operate in their relationships. They can easily notice how they talk to one another. Challenge them to see if they can guess what the teens are hoping to get out of the relationship. Is it worth it? Do they get what they want from it? Encourage them to watch the weirdness in action.

Teenagers who are seeing their friends pair up can couple-watch with an even more discerning eye. They will likely be close enough to their friends and the wide variety of emotions and relational complications they are going through to see that a romantic relationship might not be worth the trouble. Sure, they might encounter the occasional couple who seems to have their relationship in a healthy place, but that will probably be the exception. It is also likely that they are also struggling with sexual temptation, which is usually hovering beneath the surface. The key is to be able to stay in dialogue with your kids as you make observations about the relationships all around them.

Another way to talk about the reality of sexual temptation with your teens is to use a couple of pieces of construction paper as a teaching tool. Back in my youth minister days, I would illustrate the power of the sexual bond by gluing two pieces of construction paper together: one red and one blue. Once they were together, I would point out that the two pieces of paper looked like one because they were so tightly glued together. This is a great picture of the fact that *"two become one flesh"* as scripture teaches in numerous places. I would then suggest that once two people join together, it's really hard to pull them apart. (Tearing the pieces apart from one another usually results in a red and blue mess of paper. It's never a clean break.) In many ways, the baggage of previous relationships sticks with a person.

Wise parents must be diligent to communicate to their kids that romantic and sexual intimacy of even the most benign kind has the real potential to bond two people together in ways that God designed exclusively for marriage. You can lead them to see that instead of dating again and again, getting their hearts broken over and over, there is real value in saving themselves for the one that they will end up with in marriage. What's hard for most teens to grasp is that, statistically, they are very unlikely to end up marrying their high school sweethearts.

One Final Reality About Teen Relationships

There is one more reality that probably should have been mentioned at the beginning of this chapter, but it is so weighty that it stands apart from the rest. It is the one that most Christian parents ignore:

A boy/girl romance will be a distraction from your teen's relationship with God.

We tend to evaluate things in our life based upon the criteria of good versus bad. If something seems like a good thing, we embrace it. If something in our lives seems like a bad thing, we try to eliminate it. Unfortunately, that criterion is not sufficient.

1 Corinthians 10:31 contains a well-known command that gives us a better way to evaluate the stuff of our lives. *"Whether, then, you eat or drink or whatever you do, do all to the glory of God."* We are reminded that everything in our lives should propel us towards and be done for God's glory. It is the core issue of life. Thus, instead of looking at activities or relationships based on if they are good or bad, we should evaluate things based on whether or not they enable us to glorify God with our lives. We should regularly ask our kids: "Does this relationship enhance or detract from your relationship with God?"

In twelve years of working as a student minister, I cannot recall a single 15- or 16-year-old whose walk with Christ was strengthened because of a romantic relationship. In contrast, I saw hundreds upon hundreds of teenagers become distracted from the things of God by their boyfriends/girlfriends. It is the quickest and easiest way for our kids to develop a divided heart, something warned against time and time again in Scripture.

Let's make it even more personal. Take a moment to look back on the romantic relationships you had during high school. If you were a Christian during those years, reflect on the effect your boyfriends or girlfriends had on your spiritual life. If you are honest, you will probably conclude that it was a hindrance to being able to focus deeply on the things of God. This is the case with just about every young and immature relationship that our kids are likely to enter. Yet our culture encourages our kids to pursue them with abandon.

Paul wrote about this very thing in his admonition for disciples to remain single. He said in 1 Corinthians 10:32-34 that *"One who is unmarried is concerned about the things of the Lord, how he may please the Lord; but one who is married is concerned about the things of the world, how he may please his wife, and his interests are divided."*

His interests are divided. Those few words sum up just about every struggle that we will ever have as followers of Christ.

While Paul's specific admonition is about staying single, the principle also applies to dating. Too many young Christians have a desire to please God but they are too busy focusing on pleasing their boyfriends or girlfriends. Their interests are divided. Pulling them in one direction is a God they cannot see and in whom they are still learning to trust. Pulling them in another direction is a significant other who they talk to daily and to whose heart they are becoming powerfully connected. Most Christian teenagers won't admit it, but God is going to lose the battle for their hearts.

Sadly, when young people are trying to figure out the part God will play in their lives, nobody tells them this. Their daily need for Him will often become lost in their pursuit of a relationship. Their tender emotions and their desire to be loved will cloud their judgment. It is our responsibility as parents to help them to see what is going on. It is in this window of time that our role is an absolute necessity, even when we see our teenagers begin to pull away from us. In fact, it is during this season that they need us more than ever.

thirteen

Chemistry

The Addictive Power of Romantic Relationships

Every parent needs to know about a powerful little chemical called "oxytocin." As an addictive drug (of sorts), it has the potential to influence the average teenager more than alcohol, marijuana, and all other illegal substances combined. Unfortunately, most people have never even heard of it.

Do a Google search for oxytocin and more than a million results will be available. Even better, search for something a little more specific to the issues we are considering here. Google "oxytocin teenagers sex connection." When I last tried it there were almost three million results. Something is going on and parents need to know about it.

Doctors, therapists and researchers are talking more and more about the powerful biological connections that are formed when two people are physically intimate. Any parent who is striving to help their kid to be successful in her teen relationships and in her eventual marriage needs to be well-informed of what oxytocin is and how it works.

Oxytocin is known in scientific circles as "the bonding chemical."

It is secreted in both men and women, helping to create meaningful bonds and attachments to others. It also gives one a sense of euphoria in the deepest places of our mind and body. Oxytocin can be stimulated by something as simple as a really good hug with someone we love. It is also quite active in nursing women, forming a special bond between mother and child that most men can't even begin to understand.

When is oxytocin most powerfully generated? In times of sexual intimacy. It's certainly more complex than this, but one of the reasons an orgasm is so satisfying is because of the presence of oxytocin. It is what enables a husband and wife to feel so intimately connected after sex.

However, there is a dark side to oxytocin. As a simple chemical, it doesn't have any awareness of if it is working to bond a husband and a wife together or if it is bonding two people experiencing a one-night stand. But in both cases, its potential power is still the same.

God, who created everything, knew what He was doing when He created oxytocin. He created a powerful chemical bond that the human heart translates into an emotional connection with another person. It is why I have heard sex referred to as the "super glue of marriage." It bonds a husband and wife together in a way that is unique to all other human relationships.

> *Jenifer's Perspective:*
> *"Sexual intimacy is the quickest and most powerful way for a wife to connect to her husband's heart. God made it this way and it should be celebrated, not ignored or resented."*

Oxytocin plays a big part in this connection. It's the reason that God tells us to wait until marriage to experience sexual intimacy. In the context of premarital sexual activity, oxytocin has the power to undermine the very thing that it was designed to do, as this magical stuff isn't smart enough to know if the people who are secreting it are in a marriage relationship or not. It bonds any couple of any age experiencing sexual intimacy. This has tremendous implications to our kids and their dating relationships.

Most sexually active teenagers and young adults have heard plenty of lectures and public service announcements about safe sex and STDs. They are told that there are biological factors they need to consider if they don't want to get pregnant or to catch a disease. But few are aware that there are also biological factors at work that impact them emotionally and psychologically, as well.

In their excellent book - *Hooked: New Science on How Casual Sex is Affecting our Children*, - physicians Joe McIlhaney, Jr. and Freda McKissic Bush provide thorough and detailed documentation of this. They conclude that when teen couples become sexually intimate, these brain chemicals create powerful emotional bonds whose significance cannot be ignored.[1]

For parents who want to guide their kids towards healthy long-term relationships, I can identify three implications of these incredibly smart doctors' findings. When it comes to what oxytocin does and how it works, there is some bad news (two horrible implications) and there is some good news (one awesome implication).

The Bad News: Sex Makes People Stupid

Everybody knows that sex has the power to impair a person's judgment. While good sex in marriage will help you to stay crazy in love with your spouse, sexual activity outside of marriage has the potential to make you crazy in love with a complete bozo. It's why two young people who seem to have nothing in common and who are rarely seen getting along very well can't seem to break up. They are confusing lust with love and oxytocin is effectively serving as the fuel that's powering their stupidity.

In my work with hundreds of teenagers in dating relationships, something that stands out more than anything else is that sexual intimacy masks relationship flaws.

Two young people can be in a relationship that everybody in their lives can see is dysfunctional, yet they keep coming back to one another. Even if their sexual activity is relatively benign—passionate kissing, for example—there is a biological component at work beneath the surface of their relationship. Just as an addict keeps going back to the drug that he knows is ultimately not good for him, couples who are "hooked" on one another can consistently overlook the troubling parts of their relationship and stay together regardless. This can last indefinitely or until one of them finally hits a wall (or notices someone else) and ends the relationship.

More Bad News: Oxytocin Abuse Takes Its Toll

There are long-term effects of serial dating (as characterized by moving from relationship to relationship through the teen and young adult years). Those who find themselves forming emotional, sexual, and chemical connections in a long series of relationships in their developmental years will find that oxytocin begins to lose its effectiveness, its connective power. Just as a drug addict needs more and more of a substance to get the same buzz, an individual trying to find a meaningful relationship will eventually find that they cannot produce enough oxytocin to effectively help them to bond with their partner. Few people, particularly teenagers, ever consider this.

> *Jenifer's Perspective:*
> *"Too many parents think they are wise to encourage their kids to 'sow their wild oats' before they get married. They figure that this will help them to get it out of their systems before they make a long-term commitment. What it is actually doing is crippling their kids' ability to have a fulfilling marriage."*

Think of it like duct tape. If I stick a piece of duct tape to a wall and then peel it off a few months later, it will have lost some of its "stickiness." Some of the glue will likely still be on the wall. If I stick that same piece to a different wall, it's not going to stick as well. Peel it off again and put it somewhere else and it will be even less sticky. Repeat this process enough times and it's eventually not going to stick to anything. Consider this as it relates to a young person cycling through relationship after relationship on their way to marriage.

Joanna Hyatt, director of Reality Check, a sexual and relational health education program that promotes sexual integrity, puts it this way: "Studies have shown if you have multiple physical relationships that then break up, you damage your ability to form a long-term commitment. You train your brain to only do short-term. Those people who are having sex outside of marriage but still want to have a solid, successful marriage someday are making it that much harder for themselves."[2]

The Good News: God's Plan for Oxytocin

We live in a world where it is quite normal to have multiple sexual partners before one gets married. One study says that the average number of prior sexual partners for males in America is 7 and the average for females is 4.[3] I gave an anonymous online survey to couples who have attended our premarital workshops over the past few years. The average was about 4.5 previous sexual partners before meeting their spouse-to-be. Most are committed Christians.

When I speak to these young engaged couples about God's design for virginity and monogamous sex, they rarely make eye contact with me. I assume they are either zoning out because they think I'm so old-fashioned or they are saddened that they are bringing so much sexual baggage into their marriage.

Let's put God's design for oxytocin under serious scrutiny and see if it doesn't give us a renewed appreciation for God's design for sex in marriage. To do that, I will paraphrase something powerful that marriage guru Mark Gungor describes in his video teaching on "The Number One Key to Incredible Sex":

In his early, premarital sexual encounters, the typical teenage boy is likely to have an orgasmic experience that he takes immediate mental note of. But because he is young and immature, he is not able to love in a selfless way. While he may not know it, the bulk of his motivation is focused on self-gratification. All he knows is that he likes the experience and wants more of it. Thus, he begins to imprint on the sex act. He begins to learn that "sex means everything."

It's like a baby goose that sees a dog instead of its mother in its earliest days of life. The little goose imprints on the wrong "mamma" and begins to follow the dog around. Instead of learning how to fly and migrate, it learns to run in the yard. Oxytocin causes this same power of imprinting to happen to guys in their early sexual experiences. In the absence of any real substance in the relationship (no real commitment), they imprint on an experience, not a person.

For the typical teenage girl having early sexual experiences, there is often little meaning in the act. Because she ultimately desires more of an emotional connection than a sexual one, the girl hopes that physical intimacy will draw her closer to her guy. Sex is a means to an end. Tragically, a substantive emotional bond rarely happens. Apart from a committed long-term relationship, she is unable to significantly imprint on anything, neither the guy nor the sex. This is especially true if she begins to feel that the only interest the guy has in her is physical. She learns that "sex means nothing."

Now contrast that with God's plan.

Take two virgins with limited sexual experience. Let them develop a slow-simmering emotional connection based upon self-sacrificing love as modeled by Christ. Eventually, get them to an altar where, in front of their family, all their best friends, and a holy God, they pledge their life and their all to one another in a covenant "until death do us part" relationship. Then, safely in their marriage bed and with God's blessing, they have their first sexual experiences with one another. In this scenario, they are powerfully imprinting exclusively on each other, not just on the sexual act. The oxytocin that God created to connect two people (and that has been safely guarded by the couple) overwhelms them for one another.[4]

Considered in this light, God's command to *"abstain from fornication"* is less of a downer and more of a blessing. He is purposely encouraging his children to have the best sex possible: sex that perfectly ties emotional, spiritual, and physical intimacy together. Our heavenly Father truly knows what He is talking about.

Beyond just the Biblical imperatives, current social research affirms that this dynamic of marriage cannot be ignored. Published in the May 2003 edition of the *Journal of Marriage and Family*, Jay Teachman found that having just one other intimate relationship prior to marriage is linked to an increased risk of divorce.[5] In contrast, women whose intimate premarital relationships were limited to their husbands do not experience this increased risk. Sexual exclusivity between marriage partners (even before the marriage starts) creates a strength within marriage that cannot be downplayed.

When studying the data from 2008 National Survey of Family Growth, one finds a clear connection between virginity and marital success. The divorce rate for women who had just one sexual partner before marrying was 49.6%. The divorce rate over the same time period for those who married as virgins was 14.9%.[6]

This research affirms what God has been trying to tell us all along. Sexual intimacy is reserved for the marriage bed. The biological factors at play should give us as parents all the more reason to encourage our kids to save their sexuality for marriage.

Most young people don't understand the logic of God's command to wait. Sure, they may know God's opinion on the subject, but when sexual desire begins to awaken within them and they find themselves emotionally connected in a relationship, it's hard to remain convinced. With all the messages they hear that sex will make any relationship better, it's easy to start believing that, at the least, God is a bit puritanical. Or, at the worst, He is a cosmic killjoy.

Our young people will be well-served if they understand early on that there is a chemical component to the "two become one flesh" dynamic that the Bible talks about in Genesis 2:24, Matthew 19:5, and Ephesians 5:31. God is not trying to keep them from something. He is trying to protect them from messing up what He designed to be both glorious and functional in marriage. We can see that specific caution in 1 Corinthians 6:16, when Paul writes: *Do you not know that he who unites himself with a prostitute is one with her in body? For it is said, 'The two will become one flesh.'* God gives his children clear directives about handling sexual intimacy (and our oxytocin) with great care.

Sadly, it's hard to convince someone of this once they have already "drank the Kool-Aid," so to speak. Young people who are "in love" due to sexual intimacy run a high risk of losing touch with relational reality. In other words, they are not readily apt to listen to others who are convinced that the relationship is not healthy. They are, in effect, blinded by love. We must strive to train our kids in the chemical factors of love before they even get close to exploring it on their own.

How to Talk About Chemistry

Having a worthwhile conversation with our kids about the chemical components of sex and dating probably won't come easy. Children won't understand it and teenagers probably won't care. This is partially due to the fact that, as Dr. Joe McIlhaney, one of the authors of *Hooked* points out that "the prefrontal cortex, the part of the brain that has to do with judgment and reasoning has not completely developed."[7] There's a reason that rental car companies will not rent to people younger than 25.

But that doesn't mean that we shouldn't bring it up. In fact, we should make our kids mindful of it as early as possible. A simple illustration might enable even the youngest kids to grasp that there are powerful chemical factors at work in boy/girl relationships:

Somewhere along the way, your kids have probably seen a fantasy/princess movie that involved some sort of love potion given to the hero by a character in the story. I remember that *Shrek 2* had a theme like that. If taken, the potion causes the person to fall instantly and madly in love with the next person they encounter. Even if it wasn't the best person for them, the potion's power would compel them to fall in love anyway.

Using a story like that as a springboard, parents can point out the following to their kids: If they were in possession of a potion like that and they knew it had that power, they would likely handle it very carefully, making sure not to open it or touch it until they were sure that they had found the right person they wanted to be with "happily ever after." In the same way, emotional and physical intimacy (even something as benign as passionate kissing) has the exact same effect on us. It serves as something of a "love potion" that can cause us to fall in love with whomever we are with, even if they aren't good for us in other ways. Thus, kids will want to make sure they don't mess with that powerful stuff until they are sure that they are with the right person. Save your kisses, kids!

In talking with teenagers, we can come right out and put the issues on the table. Nonetheless, I would recommend that we at least make an attempt to get into their world first. One means to get there would be to look for examples of the addictive power of relationships in music.

There is a recurring theme found in the popular music of every generation. Songs often refer to the uncontrollable force that is encountered once a person falls in love. The obsessive, mind-altering power of the relationship is often described in words more appropriate to someone with a drug addiction.

As a child of the 80's, the example that my mind immediately goes to is Robert Palmer's "Addicted to Love." I can still hear him singing, "your will is not your own" while all the beautiful (yet creepy) girls played instruments in the music video. I asked my friends for other examples of this type of thing on Facebook and within a few hours they were easily able to suggest more than twenty more. Chicago sang "Hard Habit to Break." Survivor sang "High on You." Lionel Richie had a hit with "Stuck on You."

Even our parent's generation felt this. The Four Tops had a hit with "I Can't Help Myself." The uber-cheesy "You Light up My Life" captures our stupidity in love with, "It can't be wrong when it feels so right." These songs often connect with a large audience because they refer to something to which every person in love can relate.

Look for this theme in the music that your kids are listening to. When your kids are in a talking mood, ask them why they think so many songs talk about the powerful, obsessive forces found in love relationships. Transition from that to a discussion of the chemistry that is at work in our minds and bodies when we connect emotionally and physically with another. Be sure to include God's role in the process and how He designed it for marriage. He's the One responsible for it, so we need to give credit where credit is due.

If all that sounds too complicated, just make them read a few of the articles that pop up after a search for "oxytocin" in Google. That could work, too. It might remove some of the "I really don't want to discuss this with my parents" resistance that we are likely to encounter. Whatever the case, every parent must consider the chemical factors of dating and relationships as they guide their kids through these tumultuous years. There are truly powerful forces at work that we cannot afford to ignore.

fourteen

Unity

The Non-Negotiable Principle of Being "Equally Yoked"

"Missionary Dating" is a term we jokingly use when a Christian dates a non-Christian. The inference is that the Christian is going to date a lost but open-minded non-believer and eventually love them into the Christian faith. It is typically used to justify the fact that yes, we know it's not a good idea that we are dating this person, but we're hoping for the best.

It seems that everybody knows at least one person who did "missionary dating" successfully. (I think we all know the same person.) After many years of prayer and love, the lost person finally came to Christ. In contrast to that rare exception, we all know many believers who wandered away from a committed faith because they dated or married an unbeliever. This tends to happen because attempts to significantly change a person once they are married are usually fruitless. It's simply not in our human nature.

Because of that, there are few things that concern me more in the church today than how carelessly we handle the command given to us in 2 Corinthians 6:14. Paul writes: *"Do not be yoked together with unbelievers. For what do righteousness and wickedness have in common? Or what fellowship can light have with darkness?"* While the church must be fully "in the world," striving to pass truth and life to those who do not know Him, our deepest relationships should be marked by a common commitment to Christ and His Kingdom.

God gives this command as an application of a broader principle that believers are to be different and set apart from the world. After all, we have entirely different goals and a different understanding of what our lives are all about. If we connect in business or in marriage to someone whose fundamental beliefs are different than ours, the likely outcome is that our commitment to Christ and his Word will be compromised. As with oxen being "yoked together," it is impossible to successfully move a partnership forward if both parties do not hold to the same standard and share common objectives in life.

There are numerous Biblical examples of this. In scripture, when God's people got too deeply integrated into their local culture, the most likely outcome was that those who were set apart as different began to act, look and think exactly like everybody else. In most cases, it significantly watered down their impact on their world.

The truth of 2 Corinthians 6:14 is not confusing. It is not unclear. So when are we going to start taking it seriously? Why do we as parents tend to ignore the principle of being "equally yoked" when it comes to coaching our teenagers in their dating relationships? Is it because we feel like one date or a young relationship is no big deal?

There is a real threat of our kids falling in love with (and eventually marrying) someone who has vastly different values than they have. This happens because of what researchers call "sliding, not deciding" on a relationship. Too many couples find themselves in a serious relationship when it's not necessarily what they set out to have. Add sexual intimacy (of even a mild sort) and it's even harder to break the bonds that are established.

Clinical Psychologist Meg Jay sums it up this way: "Sliding into a relationship wouldn't be a problem if sliding out were as easy. But it isn't."[1] If it is so easy to get into a relationship but hard to get out of one, you would think we would take the command to be "equally yoked" a little more seriously. Perhaps the problem isn't that we don't take it seriously, but that we have such a hard time defining it.

There is not an easy litmus test to determine if a couple is "equally yoked." I mean, how "Christian" does a person need to be in order to date my teenager? Most parents I talk to classify their teenager's girlfriend or boyfriend based on where they go to church. They will say something like, "He goes to St. Mary's, so he's cool." Surely there's a better criterion than identifying with a specific church. After all, every couple will struggle with temptation and the potential of an out-of-control emotional connection. I want to make sure that the person my kid starts dating shares a set of common commitments to their faith and standards of purity. This requires a closer examination than a quick "where does he go to church?"

Perhaps a better criterion can be found in what I once heard pastor Louie Giglio say: "Relationships succeed when an awareness of God and a connectivity to God are foremost in our thinking." I want to do all I can to guide my Christian teenagers into long-lasting relationships where faithfulness to God is the priority.

If that applies to who they will marry later, then it applies to who they date now. Because, again, I know that my kids have the potential to fall in love with anybody. I want to train my kids that this is a principle for relationships in general, but in who they date specifically. As Christian parents, we should want all their relationships to push them into a deeper commitment to Christ.

Train your kids that when they notice someone who is attractive to them, their first litmus test should be: "Do they share my commitment to Christ?" Or better: "Will being with this person likely draw me closer to Christ?"

Parents Have to Think This Through

Every parent needs to thoughtfully and carefully consider this question: "In regards to my kids, when do I put a stop to an unequally-yoked relationship?" We rarely take time to think that question through to its logical conclusion. If we believe that our kids shouldn't marry an unbeliever (but we let them date them), do we have a long-term plan to end the relationship?

Do we plan to end it when they start talking about marriage? They have dated for three years and are nearing the end of their education and they start talking about the possibility of getting married. Does a parent bring it up then? "I know you guys are planning your life together, but your mother and I have a real concern about whether you should be together long-term." Good luck with that one.

Let's back it up some. Does a parent push them to end the relationship after they have dated in high school for one year? "You guys have hit the one year anniversary of your relationship, and we feel like this has gone on long enough. You're going to have to break up." That should be fun.

Let's be even more diligent. Is one date to a school dance with a friend okay and a few more dates worth considering? Then draw the line? "We see where this is going and we don't think it's a good idea for you guys to enter a relationship like this." Even that conversation could turn into World War III. It has the real potential to put the parent in a no-win situation, where they are afraid of being firm because they don't want to push their kid into rebellion. I encounter parents living with this exact tension all the time.

Instead, we would be well-advised to take a more proactive approach. Here is what I recommend: from the time your kids are in elementary school, you should declare that your family is going to hold fast to the standard of being "equally yoked." For that reason, the rule in your home will be that we do not date people who do not have the same Christian faith and practice that we do. Not a single date. Not even going to a dance "as friends." We simply will not do it. Establish that value early and then cling to it throughout the years that they are in the home. Hopefully, they will embrace it even when they leave the nest.

As we teach this principle to our kids, we must know that this is a broader issue than just dating and marriage. For the Christ-follower, being "equally yoked" means that our closest friends that we are doing life with and where there is mutual love and influence should also be Christ-followers. Yes, we should be in relationship with people from all backgrounds, but our most intimate of relationships need to have Christ in common. We would do well to start laying that groundwork early with our kids, as well.

124

How to Talk About Unity

The phrase "equally yoked" seems antiquated, but it still captures the necessity of unity better than anything else. An ancient farmer who wanted to be successful would need to make sure that the two animals pulling his plow were compatible. If he put a strong ox that was willing to walk uphill together in a yoke with a weak ox that was determined to walk downhill, the farmer would never get any work done. The two oxen's motives would be completely different.

In the same way, if two people have clearly different objectives in life, putting them together in a committed relationship is fraught with problems. Specifically, a believer's life is (in theory) surrendered to God and to the building of His Kingdom. A non-believer's life will usually be motivated by a variety of outside factors, but rarely by the calling of a Biblical worldview. This person may be a terrific and selfless person, but he does not see life through the lens of Scripture.

When two people are "unequally yoked," they are destined to experience one of two possible outcomes. One likelihood is that their lives will be full of conflict. The battle within the "yoke" of which way they will go will make both of them weary and miserable. The other possibility is that one will be strong enough to lead and influence the other to go his or her way. Unfortunately, the believer in the relationship rarely wins out.

When the discussions arise with your kids regarding what makes a potential boyfriend or girlfriend "Christian enough," the goal is not to establish some arbitrary line that every suitor must measure up to. Instead, you want to be able to honestly examine their character and motives to see if they will bring out the best in your kids. Hopefully, you will be training your kids to look for the same things you are looking for. For example, your daughters might be learning to ask things like:

- Are there clear evidences of God's activity in his life?
- Is he more interested in' pursuing God than pursuing a relationship with me?

- Does he practice spiritual disciplines?
- Does he comfortably speak of how God is at work in his life?
- Does he have a commitment to personal holiness, as evidenced by his language, his media choices, etc.?
- Can I easily see this person drawing me closer to Christ?

As you lead your kids to consider these questions when vetting a potential date, it may make you consider whether or not these things are evidenced in your kids' lives, as well. After all, how can we expect our teens' girlfriends/boyfriends to be something that our teenagers are not? There may be some work that we need to do there. Which brings me to another elephant in the room.

Parents of teenage girls and young single women must face a sobering reality. There just don't seem to be that many good Christian young men from which our daughters can choose. Beyond just "feeling like that," this is actually rooted in truth. Some studies have determined that the ratio of committed Christian young women to men is about three to two. That means that there is a significant shortage of datable Christian young men for our daughters.

It would seem that the only possible outcome for a girl who wants to eventually marry is to lower her standards. I know of many parents who have grown weary of encouraging their girls to wait for God to bring them the right kind of man.

Instead of giving up or giving in, I recommend that parents do what Voddie Baucham suggests about finding the right guy: "If you can't find one, make one." He encourages dads to look around for young men that they can disciple, coach, and push toward authentic Christian manhood. The young men in whom we invest like this may not meet every criterion we have for marrying our daughters...yet. However, they might later if we allow God to use us to refine them. It might take a serious investment of time, but our daughters are worth it.

Along those same lines, our young adult children may choose to date and even marry a person whom we know does not share our faith. If that happens, we would be wise to prayerfully look for opportunities to point them to Christ. It is never too late for a parent to offer influence and for God to work. Never lose hope, even if there is struggle along the way.

We all know of couples who are in conflict because of clear and marked differences in their Christian commitment. While the marriages are difficult, the greater loss might be that the children in those homes will be less likely to embrace the Christian faith that their parents can't seem to agree on. This compromised legacy is exactly why God commands us to not be unequally yoked together with unbelievers.

Do not forget how most of those couples got there. Their marriages were formed years ago because an intimate relationship was established. Intimate relationships happen when people date. Dates happen when young people flirt with and pursue someone whom they like. It all starts at that basic, seemingly innocent place. It is for this reason that we must diligently teach our children that "equally yoked" includes the first date. The line must be drawn somewhere, so why not there?

fifteen

Accountability

Providing Meaningful Oversight to Our Dating Teens

Go on YouTube and do a search for "hidden camera bad dog." It will take several days to watch all the hidden camera videos people have made to capture what their dogs do once the people leave. Apparently, dog lovers around the world share a common problem: when they are home, their pets behave themselves. When they leave, their dogs get into all sorts of trouble. They get into the trash, chew on expensive shoes, and climb onto furniture they know they are not supposed to. The pattern among our canine friends is that when nobody is looking, they get into trouble. When left alone, the worst comes out of them.

I hate to make a comparison of dogs to our teenage kids, but at a fundamental level, the illustration holds up. When our kids enter a boy/girl relationship and there is no parental oversight, there is the real potential for bad things to happen.

My experience is that every generation of young people holds to the default position that their parents were born yesterday. They feel that their parents are generally clueless and that they (the teens) can get away with just about anything because their parents are so easily deceived. Perhaps kids come to believe this so readily because their parents are naïve or entirely disengaged from the activities and challenges of the typical teenager. This is not good. As parents, we need to be clued in to what our kids are up to. I am not suggesting that we sneak around and spy on our kids. On the contrary, our kids should clearly know of our desire to be "in the know."

My 17-year-old once told me it is hard being my daughter. She describes her friends' parents as being entirely oblivious as to what their kids are involved in. They get into all sorts of trouble and their parents don't have a clue. She went on to say that while she doesn't always like my awareness and oversight into her life, she appreciates and values it. It makes her feel safe and loved. Isn't that what we all want to aim for as parents?

What does accountability of our kids' dating relationships look like? We will explore that a bit here, but it might be easier to explain up front what it doesn't look like. While I always laugh at the humorous posts that are emailed to me about the "rules for dating my daughter," they have the real potential to cause us to miss the point. We end up with nothing more than a few funny comments about "cleaning our guns" when the boy comes to pick up our daughter. If all we do is make jokes but do not offer any substantive protection and accountability for our kids, we are failing our children. Instead, our kids need a measure of accountability and oversight in at least three areas of their dating lives.

1. Parents Should Give Input About Who Their Kids Date

Parents have permission and even a solemn responsibility to give input into who their kids connect with in a romantic way. I'm not suggesting that we return to a time of arranged marriages, only that parents are involved in the discussion. With all the avenues of digital communication, it is relatively easy for a teenager to be in a relationship with someone without his or her parents' knowledge. This is extremely hazardous and bypasses the very reason that God wants parents to be involved: to offer accountability and oversight. From the earliest age possible, our kids should be taught that their mom and dad have a vote (and even veto power) on any and all romantic relationships.

2. Parents Need to Interact With Them as They Date

Parents should strive to spend as much time with their dating teens as possible. I am not suggesting that we be an ever-present chaperone as they date, though we could make a pretty good argument for that. Instead, my goal is to get to spend time with them as a couple, coming to better know this young person who has expressed an interest in my teenager. Making my home available for them to spend time there is the most practical means to make this happen. Family meals or movie nights give us opportunities to get to know the person my teenager is interested in. In addition, having them around allows me to see how they interact with one another and enables me to know how to coach them.

> *Jenifer's Perspective:*
> *"I want to have a positive influence on anyone who enters a relationship with my kids, even as friends. I want them to be able to say that they have a better relationship with God because of the time they have spent with us."*

3. Parents Should Influence Both of Them as They Date

Overly romantic relationships between immature teenagers have a huge downside and should be entered into very cautiously. Nonetheless, within some clearly-defined boundaries, they can serve as opportunities to train our older teenagers on how to interact with the opposite-sex. Our sons can learn to be gentlemen and our daughters to be ladies. This typically happens in the context of our homes and with some firm parameters regarding emotional and physical intimacy. Our hope is that it will give our older teens a safe environment to get to know someone better. (In the case of our oldest daughter, it led to a marriage.) This will not happen automatically. These lessons need to be carefully steered by parents who are exerting influence and giving parameters for the relationship as it evolves.

130

How to Talk About Accountability

I used to work for a pastor who loved to integrate pop-culture phrases into his conversations. For example, when he had some insight or insider information on something I was involved in, he would always say, "I know what you did last summer." Quoting the title of a goofy horror movie, his point was to say, "I know what you did. I know what you are up to. I know what you are capable of."

Our kids should always have the sense that we know what they are doing and what they are capable of. This sense should not come from the fact that we are secretly spying on them, but on the fact that we are openly talking with them about their friends and potential relationships. We are giving input into who they date, interacting with them as they date, and exerting influence as they date. The goal is to be a loving and ever-present source of accountability that can confidently say "I know what you did last summer."

The foundational place to start this is in what Dennis Rainey calls "the interview." He writes of this extensively in his excellent book *Interviewing Your Daughter's Date.* It practically plays out when she is a teenager, but I recommend that dads of preschool girls read it so they can start preparing their daughters for what they can expect as they get older.

The crux of what Rainey teaches is that if someone wants to date my daughter (or even my son), they have to go through me first. In the case where dad isn't involved, mom can step in instead. In our family, my kids knew that if anyone pursues them, wants to go out with them, or even wants to invite them to a school dance, they have to talk to me first. This mandatory step accomplishes a few good things even before the "interview" takes place.

One good thing that it provides is a way to filter out the riff-raff. A guy was pursuing one of my girls and she told him that he had to call me to talk more about it. It turns out that he wasn't the least bit interested in doing that. He thought that was a dumb idea. My daughter recognized that if the guy wasn't willing to have a simple talk with her father, then he wasn't worth dating.

Another simple thing that this process offers for our girls is a simple and quick way out of an awkward situation. One of my girls was studying by herself at a bagel shop and a young employee there started flirting with her. She was rather annoyed but tried to be polite. When he finally asked for her number, she wrote down my number instead, telling him that he had to call me first. He left her alone and I never heard from him.

This process also sets the standard for my sons. If one of my boys wants to pursue a girl, he knows that he has to talk to her dad first. I'm not going to expect this of the guys who are interested in my girls but not expect a similar process from my boys. This gives the girl's dad a measure of confidence from the beginning of a possible relationship. It also communicates that my son is interested in coming under the dad's authority as the protector of his daughter. Most guys today would never dream of doing this, so it makes for a great first-impression on the dad.

So what does the interview look like? Not actually an interview (no resumes or applications change hands), it is more of a conversation. The goal is for me as a dad to get to know the guy, make sure he is a good fit, and to clearly communicate expectations and parameters for the relationship. By the time it is over, I want to have accomplished the following:

1. Have a Good Idea of Who The Guy Is

At a bare minimum, I will want to know about his family, his faith, and his intentions. I do more than ask about if and where he goes to church. I ask about his relationship with God or about what God has been teaching him in recent days. This might give me insight into his spiritual maturity or understanding. If, under the Spirit's leadership in my life, I come to the conclusion that he will not be right for my daughter, I will need to let him know that. Of course, I try hard not to be a jerk about it. In fact, this may be the perfect chance to invest in a young man who doesn't have a clue how to grow up spiritually but who shows some potential. Perhaps I will be the man who can help him with that.

2. Communicate How My Family Views Dating

Obviously, this will be unique for each family. In addition, the feel of the conversation will be different depending on the girl's age. A guy pursuing my daughter at 15 will get an entirely different talk than the guy who is pursuing her at 21. At the bare minimum, I will seek to let any guy know that I am held accountable before God for the care of my daughter until that time that I can walk her down an aisle and surrender her to the care of her husband. If I let a guy take my car out for a few hours, I would give him some clear parameters on what was expected. Because my kids are vastly more valuable to me than my car, he can expect me to give him some non-negotiable parameters regarding what this relationship will be and will not be.

3. Share Expectations for The Relationship

We need to be as specific as possible in this. If I am not comfortable with my daughter being in a heavily emotional relationship yet, I tell the boy straight up. When my daughter went to a school dance as a sophomore with a friend, I had every confidence that they truly were "just friends." Still, it did not stop me from looking her friend in the eye and making my expectations crystal clear. "I am glad that you guys are going to this dance, but I am not at the point where I am comfortable with my daughter being in a boy/girl relationship. Are we clear on that?" He said that he was and that was that. Better to make it clear in the beginning than have to reel something in later on.

4. Be Clear About Physical Boundaries

This is the point where I communicate that I am not a clueless parent. I want to let the boy know that I know what he is capable of. I want him to know that I am aware that sexual temptation is a real possibility in every teen relationship.

I tell the young man as clearly as I possibly can: "I like you and want you to spend time with my daughter. But at no time are you to put your hands or your lips on my daughter. That is my expectation. If, at a later date, you find you want to do either of those things, then you can come talk to me about it. For now, I want you to get to know my daughter without the complication of physical affection, because physical intimacy will make you both stupid."

Is this conversation comfortable? Of course not. Is it critical to providing my kids with the accountability they need? Absolutely.

5. Assure Him That I Will Be Talking to Him Some More

I remind him that this is not a one-time conversation. He can expect me to check in on him from time to time to see how the relationship is going, but also to confirm that he is living up to the expectations I just gave him. From there on out, I bring the same kind of care and accountability I brought to the interview to my ongoing oversight of the relationship. I want to consistently let my kids know that I care enough about them to "stay all up in their business." Ultimately, I want them to know that I love them enough to keep watching out for them.

For the dad who insists on cleaning his guns when a potential date comes over, that's fine. However, an honest conversation with a concerned adult who asks blunt questions and sets clear expectations is what our kids really need.

sixteen

Social Media

Setting Parameters on Their Digital World

Rebecca is a typical 15-year-old living in the suburbs of a major American city. She has never known a world where digital communications and technology were not readily available. Consider her typical day:

The alarm on her smart phone wakes her up for school on Monday. She immediately checks her phone for texts that she may have gotten after going to sleep. She responds to all of them immediately. After getting ready for school, she takes a "selfie" picture in the mirror and posts it on Instagram. While eating her breakfast, she checks Facebook for any updates and to make sure she did her homework assignment correctly. On the way to school, she gets and sends a total of fifteen different texts with four different people. Before class, she looks to see how many people "liked" her photo on Instagram.

During the school day, Rebecca will "tweet" six times, find out on her smartphone that her best friend is now "Facebook official" with the guy she asked to prom, and send/receive more than 50 texts, most of which say, "what r u doing?"

Once her school day is over, she will check Facebook again to see what her friends are doing, to find out about homework assignments on class Facebook groups, and to see pictures that everyone is posting of the weekend party that she didn't get invited to. She will (unknowingly) evaluate her worth as an individual based upon how many people "liked" her Instagram photo, her snarky "tweets," and her Facebook comments. That evening, she might eat dinner with her family, but her phone is close by and she can easily sneak a dozen texts in during one fifteen-minute meal. She can also simultaneously stay updated on three different social media sites while writing a paper on the French Revolution. Multi-tasking comes very easy for her.

As she lies in bed, she carries on five different text conversations and uses FaceTime on her smartphone to talk to the boy that she likes but who she hasn't declared her affections for just yet.

By the time she gets to sleep on that typical Monday night, Rebecca has sent and received 200 texts, posted 15 times on Twitter, commented on 30 different status updates on Facebook, put five pictures on Instagram (including two of what she ate that day), all using a device the size of a cassette tape that has more processing power than all the computers NASA used to put a man on the moon. Digital technology and connectivity truly dominates, even facilitates, her life. And sadly, she may even think that she actually has 850 friends.

The Bible does not talk about technology, but it does have a lot to say about what we put before our eyes and in our minds. While digital technology has afforded the most significant quantum leap in communications in our history, it has also brought a non-stop flow of information and messages to our hearts and minds.

Chris, the middle school minister at my church, knows more about this stuff than anybody I know, regularly teaching workshops for parents on teens and technology. His observation is that the biggest issue that many parents miss is that our kids are connected to their peers 24 hours a day, 7 days a week. Compare that with what we had when we were young. We saw friends at school or church, we could hang out with close friends at other times, and we could use the family phone (probably with tight boundaries as it seems dad was always "waiting on a call"). But there were windows of time when we disconnected from our friends and were forced to interact with our family.

In contrast, our kids are ALWAYS connected to their peers. They are constantly texting, regularly checking for updates on social media, and ever mindful of what everyone else is doing. This is very significant in that constant connection equates to constant influence from peers and a never-ending stream of temptations from the world around them.

In a similar way, these technologies greatly affect our ability to know and influence who our kids are connecting with. Before cell phones and social networking, a parent could expect some measure of interaction with their kids' friends. They would likely get to know them because they were physically present. Not so much anymore. With digital "friends," we may be the last person to know who our kids are interacting with. This has huge implications to boy/girl relationships. Twenty years ago, a parent would typically know who his teen was talking to on the phone. Now it is possible for a relationship to exist that is almost entirely digital.

> *Jenifer's Perspective:*
> *"Young people will say things in a text that they would not say in person. When sitting at a keyboard (particularly late at night), a false sense of safety is present that encourages boldness in communication. This has the potential to fast-track an unhealthy intimacy between a boy and a girl that is not usually rooted in emotional maturity."*

Parents may see the digital world that our kids live in as a foreign environment, one that we will never understand. There may be a temptation to simply "let them do their thing." That would be careless of us. Because it is where they live (and because it truly is their primary means of interaction), we must be wise enough to understand it and provide some measure of guidance within it. If we do not, then we have surrendered our kids' most significant stream of information and influence over to those who do not have their best interests at heart.

Children today are not having to learn to function in a digital world. It is all they have ever known. They are fully immersed. At two years old, my daughter was able to successfully navigate my iPhone. At four she learned to surf the web. These things are as natural as breathing to our children. If we fail early on to set clear parameters on the use of and accountability within their digital world, the rules we establish when they are teenagers will be met with incredible resistance.

Consider the parent who, three months after giving their middle school daughter a cell phone, sees on their phone bill that she was sending 5,000 texts a month. Just watch the sparks fly as they tell her that they will be restricting her to just 500 monthly texts. This is a conflict that will not end well.

It is far better to start by letting our kids know when they are very young that all technology including phones, the computer, social media, etc. are not rights, but privileges. As their parents, we get to control them and determine how they will work and when our children have access to them.

We will be allowed to know their passwords for their accounts. We will get to monitor how much time they spend using them. Just as we have a reasonable amount of oversight regarding who they hang out with, we will have the right to put parameters on who they will connect with in the digital world.

When our kids are young, they are not likely to make a big issue about the boundaries that we set for them with their technology. They will get used to these parameters as normal. As they gain more access to digital interaction with people (through social media, texting, etc.), the rules won't be a shock to their system. What we want to avoid is our kids developing a mindset that says their parents have control over their physical world but that they can do what they please in the online world.

Remember that, as parents, we are allowed to communicate the following to our kids: "I have provided these services and they are to be used at my discretion." The earlier we can squelch feelings of entitlement in our kids regarding their technology, the better.

138

How to Talk About Social Media

As with everything on the internet, there are good and bad parts of social media. While there are different tools and technologies that are appropriate for different ages, we should not make the mistake of forbidding our kids from using them. They are not going away.

I like what Mark Matlock says in his book *Raising Wise Children*: "If in my fear I refuse to allow them to participate in the technology that is now integral in daily life, I would lose the opportunity to show them how to use that technology wisely in a way that honors Christ."[1]

Ultimately, our goal should be to be aware of how our kids are using technology and to keep a healthy measure of communication and oversight as they use it. Just as with driving, the more they prove their trustworthiness, the more freedoms we can give them. Here are six keys to staying engaged and connecting with our kids about technology.

1. Be Informed About What is Out There

I could list all the websites and social media tools that kids are using to connect with each other today, but each month delivers a potential new platform. The landscape is changing that fast and parents cannot afford to be oblivious. As of this writing, more and more teens are ditching Facebook in favor of microblogging sites like Twitter and Instagram. This is probably due to the fact that their grandmothers are getting on Facebook.

The hot thing today is Snapchat, which allows users to send quick bursts of data (pictures or video) that are immediately deleted. Some watchdogs are warning that this app is "made for sexting." Sites that allow kids to post questions and get anonymous answers from their peers are particularly troubling. More on that in a minute. The technological landscape changes quickly, so stay current!

With that in mind, it would be pointless to give all the sites that are out there because they change so fast. Google "social media sites for teens" and you are likely to find some good information. Or you could ask a 20-year-old you trust.

2. Know What Sites Your Teens Are Using

At the bare minimum, we need to know what social media platforms our kids frequent. We also need to educate ourselves on how they work. If there are privacy settings that keep unwanted people from seeing their information, then take full advantage of them. Facebook (and others) have caught some flack for being pretty lax in their parental controls, so we have to be diligent to provide some intentional oversight with our kids.

There's nothing wrong with parents requiring that our kids "friend" us on Facebook or let us "follow" them on Twitter. They probably won't be thrilled about this, but it's a reasonable expectation. Kids need to know that their digital world isn't a place free from parental influence and accountability. They need this from us. To be clear: it is okay to periodically ask your kids what sites they are using. Make them show you around and put whatever controls in place you see fit.

3. Set Guidelines for Interacting With the Opposite sex

Most young people today have parents who give them very few (if any) boundaries for interacting with the opposite-sex. With so many means of communication (cell phones, texting, social networking, etc.) our kids are interacting with others all the time. Without any guidelines given, they will come to assume that they have free rein to interact with anyone they want at any time they want.

Like no generation before them, our kids see "being connected" as a given that has no boundaries whatsoever. This will certainly affect the habits they will eventually develop as it relates to the opposite-sex.

4. Have the "Digital Footprint" Conversation

It never ceases to amaze me how many stories I hear of good kids doing dumb things online. Girls are sending racy pictures of themselves to their boyfriends. Guys are posting questionable pictures or statements on Facebook or Instagram.

It's a fundamental truth that teenagers are not yet able to fully understand the long-term implications of the choices they make today. To make matters worse, this generation has access to a digital world that has the potential to display their bone-headed choices (and the consequences) to the world, at large. The bad news is that, once they put something out there, it's hard to get it back. Parents MUST talk about this with their kids.

We need to inform and then remind them of the significance of what they put online and where they go on the internet. We need to tell them that anything they do has the potential to be permanent. Even though we may presume that our kids aren't foolish enough to "sext" someone, we need to tell them not to anyway. (One in four teens have done it at least once. That's a lot of foolish teens.)

Remind them that colleges, employers, and others are regularly looking online to learn about the character of applicants. The stakes are very high, indeed. Give them reasons for the rules and then put clear boundaries in place, making it clear that online use (either on the computer or phone) is a privilege and that there are consequences for irresponsible behaviors.

5. Be on Guard for Digital Abuse

My heart breaks every time I hear a story on the national news about the suicide of a teenager who was bullied on the internet. Because the abuse takes place in a public forum for all to see, it can be far more destructive than a hurtful word in the hallway at school. Wise parents should be on the lookout for any signs of digital abuse, because it can show up in subtle ways.

Girls (far more than guys) will often put pictures of themselves online. Commonly called "selfies," these pictures are often accompanied by a caption that says something to the effect of "*Like* if you think I'm pretty." While she may be looking for and even get some positive affirmation, there is always the possibility that she will get a cruel comment from someone who wants to hurt her. Or she may hear "crickets," which might have an altogether different effect on her self-esteem.

Even worse is the development of Q&A social networking sites such as "ask.fm." These sites give users the chance to post a question and then get anonymous responses from their "friends." As cruel as middle school girls are prone to be, sites like this in the wrong hands can be absolutely brutal. As a parent who cares about his own kids, I would strongly encourage parents to ban sites like these from their homes.

6. Provide Oversight of Technology Use

Let me affirm once again that parents have every right to get "all up in their kids' business" regarding their use of technology. That will probably mean putting some clearly-defined boundaries in place. Note that this was placed last on this list because the conversations we have with our kids are far more important than the rules. However, rules and oversight are still necessary.

Parents should talk with their kids about accountability regarding the frequency and timing of cell phone usage. Most cell carriers can limit the number of texts per billing cycle and that may come in handy for kids who are chronic texters. We can also set time frames for when the cell can be used, and simply placing a basket in the kitchen where all kids' phones go at a predetermined time (say ten o'clock), works well, too.

This will be covered in greater detail in the next chapter, but an internet filter or monitoring software should be found in every home. While we cannot completely block everything bad from getting on our home computers, it is a good idea to have some system for deterring it at some level. Be warned: our filters will not always be with our kids. More than just putting technology in place to guard our kids' hearts and minds, we must place a far greater priority on helping our kids to integrate the God-honoring value that explicit content is not good for them.

Parents should lay down this parameter as early as possible, but our kids should know that we have every right to check their phone or their computer at any time. It is not a daily event, but I occasionally check my kids' phones to see who (and what) they are texting. Again, I have "friended" my teens on Facebook so I can occasionally scan their wall to check on the things they and their friends are talking about.

Parents need to have a measure of input and control over these issues, giving more freedom as our kids show they are capable and trustworthy. What we cannot afford to do is to live oblivious of our kids' activities and connections in the digital world. There are far too many avenues for unhealthy relationships and interactions for us to remain unaware.

The good news is that our God is Lord over all creation, including things devised by man such as the computer and the smartphone. Just as we look to Him for leadership in every other area of our lives, we can look to Him for guidance and wisdom as we coach our kids to use these tools wisely. If we will only look to Him, He promises to lead us. With the world quickly changing and new technologies always developing, we need His leadership more than ever.

seventeen

Pornography

The "M" Word Now Will Impact a Marriage Later

A few years ago, Jenifer and I were in the middle of leading a few hundred parents of teenagers through a teaching series we created called "Let's Talk About Sex." We wanted to cover a variety of dating and sex issues as they related to teenagers, and that's the best title we could come up with at the time. (If you are like me, that title always serves to put that catchy Salt-n-Pepa tune from the early 90's in my head. If that just happened to you, I sincerely apologize.)

On a Saturday night we encountered a middle-aged couple at a restaurant. They had heard our first talk the previous Sunday morning and were looking forward to the rest of our teaching. Specifically, they were anxious for direction on how to put some parameters on their son's dating relationship.

I assured them that we would cover that, but that we would also address plenty of other significant issues, as well. Curious, they asked me to elaborate. I mentioned a few things, but specifically zeroed in on an issue specifically related to sons...an issue of a "self-gratifying" nature. Apparently, my desire to be discrete in a crowded restaurant wasn't getting my point across because they stared at me with blank expressions on their faces. I finally had to bluntly say, "We will spend some time talking about masturbation."

They gave an uncomfortable laugh and then the woman immediately said something like, "Well, we'd rather he do THAT than be intimate with his girlfriend."

I certainly understand this mom's sentiment, but I'm not sure that I totally agree with her. While I am pretty sure that no guy ever got a girl pregnant while masturbating, it is potentially just as risky to her teenager's spiritual and sexual health. This is especially true as it relates to the effects it might have on his or her marriage down the road. It is far from harmless.

Masturbation used to be something of a taboo subject. When most people from our generation were young, it was not often talked about. Today, it has entered the mainstream, particularly in the realm of entertainment. Ever since *American Pie* made nearly $250 million at the box office in 1999, and Jerry Seinfeld and his friends had their "contest" on primetime TV, it has become both the brunt of jokes and a comfortable topic among young people.

Likewise, issues like masturbation or sexual addiction used to be relegated to the male gender. Not so any more. There are increasing numbers of young women who are struggling with these habits and tendencies. Recent studies have shown that one out of every three people who view pornography are women.[1] Most of them are young and at an age where they are establishing their perspectives of sex.

To make matters worse, masturbation has become powerfully linked to pornography in our modern society. Readily available explicit material has provided an endless supply of fuel for what used to be a vice that was rarely talked about by most people. The typical young person gets their first taste of explicit material when they are very young. Many (especially as they enter the pubescent years) will begin to seek it out. Many of them get hooked. And they stay hooked.

While pornography and masturbation are not mentioned in the Bible, Jesus tells us in no uncertain terms that lust is a serious sin. In Matthew 5:28 He said, *"Anyone who looks at a woman lustfully has already committed adultery with her in his heart."* I have yet to find anyone who can view porn without lusting. As with every other sin,

Jesus is reminding us that lust has significant consequences on our relationships with others. It's about time that we started believing Him.

Let us make no mistake: we are talking about an issue that has the potential to quickly move from curiosity to interest to full-blown addiction. "Researchers have proven what addicts have known for a long time: that sexual activity can provide a high equal to crack cocaine. The neurochemical process is identical!"[2] We should take this just as seriously as we do our desire to keep our kids away from drugs, especially since illicit material is far more accessible than most drugs are.

The impact of this addiction may manifest itself in some immediate ways. Some people may become withdrawn and less confident. Others may become more arrogant and aggressive. All of them will experience turbulence in their relationship with God. The guilt and shame associated with habitual sin is likely to lead them to experience an overwhelming sense of defeat in their spiritual lives.

Talking specifically about boys, James Dobson suggests that parents should not demonize this sin, as it only serves to add to the shame and guilt that he already feels.[3] On this point, I agree. This sin is no worse than any other. Loading our kids up with shame over something they likely feel immense guilt about already doesn't help. But we must not turn a blind eye to it, thinking that it's healthy and acceptable behavior for our kids. Giving them an awareness of the issues and ramifications should be a key part of our strategy.

One concern that is often overlooked is the long-term effect a pornography and masturbation habit will have once a young man enters marriage. What parents might easily write off as a "phase" their son is going through actually has the potential to create a significant stronghold in his life that will not be fully realized until adulthood.

I have counseled many married men who have confessed to me some type of sexual addiction. In every case, their obsession started when they were teenagers. Most of them were confident that getting married would make the addiction go away. They were certain that, once they had a sexual outlet with the woman they loved, their attraction to pornography would subside. In every case, they were wrong. This is not a behavior that men (or women) are prone to grow out of naturally and it doesn't go away once a person gets married. In fact, it makes things much more ugly as the impact is no longer just private and internal. It spills over onto the people closest to them.

As with many of the other issues we are exploring here, the problems of youth do not automatically disappear once a person grows up and walks down the aisle.

Wise parents must recognize this. They will have enough foresight to realize that their kids will likely one day be married adults. They will do all they can to keep their kids far away from the stuff. They will take this job very seriously.

Training Boys to Be Lazy, Unromantic Husbands

Imagine a young man who learns to gratify himself via explicit images at 14. He makes a normal habit of this for 10 or 12 years. He learns, through experience, that sexual satisfaction requires nothing of him. The girl is always interested. She is always "in the mood." He can find immediate satisfaction whenever he wants. Sex is easy.

Then, imagine this young man entering a covenant marriage relationship. He soon discovers that the girl requires something of him. For intimacy to happen, there must be time, love, attention, romance, and an investment into the relationship. It's more work than he has ever had to do before. Once the honeymoon is over, he may decide that it's just not worth the effort. He has developed a ten-year tendency towards sexual laziness that is incredibly hard to overcome.

With that in mind, it could be argued that the most widespread impact of the porn industry is the destruction of sexual intimacy in marriage due to lazy husbands. Of course, no one would argue that the *most horrible* impact of porn can be found in violent sexual crimes. I am in no way downplaying that. However, for every case of sexual assault, I would imagine that there are hundreds of marriages that are struggling because of men who have been conditioned by porn and have no clue how to love a real woman. Even those who try may be unsuccessful because they have so programmed their bodies to respond to self-stimulation that they find it challenging to perform with their spouse.

According to author Naomi Wolf, "The onslaught of porn is responsible for deadening male libido in relation to real women, and leading men to see fewer and fewer women as 'porn worthy.'"[4]

I saw this first hand in a newlywed man I met for breakfast a few years ago at IHOP. He was a fit, good-looking, and successful man in his late 20's. He was less than a year into his marriage and he and his wife were already struggling. At issue was the fact that, even though he claimed to be a very sexually driven man, he wasn't interested in being intimate with his wife. She had gained some weight since their wedding day and, according to him, she was no longer attractive.

With a straight face, he shared with me how he was trying to work on the problem by looking at pornographic images of overweight girls to see if he could get into it. Obviously, I was stunned. I suggested the possibility of connecting with his wife sexually, not because she looked perfect, but because she is his wife and they have a beautiful marriage to celebrate intimately in the bedroom. He stared back at me as if to say he had no idea what I was talking about. Our porn-filled world is truly having a significant impact on young men today.

Does this sound unbelievable? Its not. At least it isn't to the regular stream of couples I encounter who tell me that this is exactly why their marriages are unraveling. The husband is hooked on the stuff and the wife feels unloved, inadequate and betrayed. Can God change their hearts and bring them victory? Of course, He can. The last time I checked, He is still in the business of doing exactly that. However, the road will not be easy.

Most parents are already convinced of the power that pornography can have over young men, in general. For many parents of boys, there might be a reluctance to believe that it can happen to their son, in particular. If that is the case, we would do well to remember that this issue is more widespread than ever in today's youth culture.

I once heard pastor and author Mark Driscoll say that "the only things that most 19-year-old boys know how to do are play video games and masturbate." This always makes me laugh, but it's not very funny.

Not too long ago, the student minister at a large church informally surveyed a group of 11th- and 12th-grade-boys that were in his discipleship group. In many ways, these ten boys were the leaders, the "best of the best" within a student ministry of 500 teenagers. He specifically asked them about their struggles with pornography. Every one of them confessed that it was a significant temptation, and that it often got the best of them. Every one of them. Sadly, these were the spiritual pacesetters within the ministry.

This is an issue affecting our kids, not just somebody else's.

Dr. Chap Clark of the Fuller Youth Institute says that 60% of teen boys in America are addicted to porn. He defined "addicted" as 3 visits per week to a porn site at one hour per visit. He also suggested that in upper-class areas where internet access was highly prevalent, the number might be as high as 80%.[5]

If I knew that 60 to 80% of the teenagers in my community were addicted to meth or heroin, I would be aggressively militant in my attempt to help my kids stay clean. We would talk about it. Often. I also would probably get a police-trained drug dog as our family pet. There would be random drug tests several times per week. I would take this threat very seriously.

We must take the porn issue just as seriously. We must get comfortable talking about it. We have to tell our boys (and even our girls) that it has the power to destroy their lives. We must teach them some practical steps to face the temptation that they will encounter on a daily basis, perhaps for the rest of their lives.

This is certainly a topic that we want to avoid. It is so vile in nature that we are reluctant to introduce it to our children for fear that we will steal their innocence unnecessarily. This is a noble and good intention, but with most kids seeing porn for the first time in elementary school, it is probably not realistic.

How to Talk About Pornography

When your child has something pop up on the computer, sees something on YouTube, or has a friend show him something explicit, he is likely to be intrigued by it. Egged on by his friend, his curiosity will likely get the best of him and he will look. If the pattern of most men is true, the longer he lingers, the greater the likelihood he will want to look some more. Once his innocence is lost, it is impossible to fully gain it back. So your child desperately needs to develop an opinion about porn long before he encounters it.

Your son or daughter needs to know enough that he or she can be on the lookout for it.

If you share with your child that, sadly, we live in world where porn not only exists but is quite prevalent and is accepted by many, there is a greater chance that his opinion of it will be established from a young age. He will know that it is dangerous and that it has the power to mess up his life. He will know this because his dad or mom told him.

The key is to talk about it before your kids see it for the first time. If a family lives a relatively sheltered existence, they might be able to have this conversation at the same time as "the talk." That's what I have done with my boys. Early elementary school is not too early for most.

Remember, this is not just an issue for our boys. More and more young women are dealing with addictions that got started when they were very young.

For Younger Kids

If there is still a measure of innocence in your kids (so you hope), you can simply tell them that they might at some time encounter something on the internet that has people with their clothes off. You can tell them in no uncertain terms that it is something they will want to run from for several different reasons.

First, it runs contrary to the basic rule that we need to keep our private parts private. Just as we have taught our children to keep themselves covered up, God wants all people to guard their bodies.

Secondly, it is damaging to the people who look at it. Just like a drug, looking at pictures or videos of people who are naked can be highly addictive. In fact, dopamine is released in the brain and it has a very similar effect on our bodies as taking drugs does. In no uncertain terms, we must communicate to our children that looking at this stuff has the power to significantly mess them up.

Thirdly, it doesn't honor the people in the pictures or videos. Their lives are very sad in that they have chosen to let someone take their pictures in that way. We need to pray for those people, not look at them in their foolish and tragic behavior.

In the midst of any coaching, we should tell our kids that it is okay to be curious. God wired men and women to be interested in the opposite-sex. However, God has also placed parameters in our lives for our good. Looking at others in this way is harmful to our hearts and minds.

Another critical thing to tell our younger kids when we talk to them about porn is exactly what we want them to do if and when they encounter it. If we have been diligent to tell them that it is out there, they are likely to know it when they see it. Tell them that it is okay for them to tell you if and when they happen to see someone with their clothes off.

You might say something like: "You may see something inappropriate while on the computer or at a friend's house. Or you might stumble onto something while channel surfing on the TV. If and when that happens, I want you to tell me. You won't be in trouble and you won't be punished. I just want to know what you ran into and to be able to talk with you about it. You can let me know and it will be okay."

For Older Kids

With kids who are more sexually aware (this includes both teenage boys AND girls) you can go into a lot more detail of how dangerous porn is. While it might be an awkward conversation, most kids are weary of facing this issue on their own. There are plenty of kids who want the chance to discuss seriously what they have seen, since the world of pornography is wide open to them but is rarely addressed in any helpful forum whatsoever.

You can share how severely porn can mess them up in the here and now. You can describe how highly addictive it is and how easily it is to become enslaved by it. Most men and women who have a

151

sexual addiction (and there are many) will admit that it started when they were young teenagers.

You can tell them that there is a high likelihood that their brain will remember a great deal of what they see. Once images are viewed, they can be potentially stored away in the brain forever. In her book, *For Women Only,* Shaunti Feldhahn calls this the "visual rolodex."[6] This is particularly true for men.

We can tell them that it will affect their ability to interact in healthy ways with others. Marnia Robinson wrote in *Psychology Today* that as previous porn users cut back on their habit, "their desire to connect with others surges. So does their confidence, their ability to look others in the eye, their sense of humor, their perception of their 'manliness,' their concentration, their optimism, their judgment, their attractiveness to potential mates, and so forth."[7] One teenager expressed the debilitating power of porn in this way: "Porn has been so normalized that anyone objecting to it now is just going to be laughed at. I think we need to hear again about how pornography threatens intimacy."[8]

Finally, we can describe how it has become the number one tool that Satan uses to build shame in teenagers and to cripple them from becoming people who walk intimately with God. Satan does this by dumping loads and loads of condemnation and guilt on them for their sin, but he makes them think it is coming from God. The typical result is that those who are dabbling in porn begin to distance themselves from God, missing out on the grace and restoration He offers, all the while becoming further entrenched in their behavior. They forget that *"there is now no condemnation for those who are in Christ."* (Romans 8:1)

John Piper addressed this very thing to a group of more than 50,000 college students a few years ago at the Passion conference. He suggested that Satan ensnares young people with sexual sin because it has the unique power to convince them that they are ineligible for God's work. That somehow their guilt and shame is too great for God to overlook. This is a lie that is straight from the pit of hell and we would do well to remind our kids of that very thing.

If one of your teenagers admits to a significant struggle with lust, he or she will need guidance to find restoration and victory at the cross. We address this in detail in chapter 22.

Skills We Can Teach Kids of Every Age

Our kids WILL encounter pornography. It is not a matter of "if" but "when." One parent of an 8-year-old commented that with more young kids having smartphones, the school bus has become the most dangerous place for innocent eyes. With that in mind, there are a couple of essential skills that every person needs to have to encounter and combat the temptations of pornography.

First of all, kids can be trained to "bounce their eyes." In *Every Man's Battle* Stephen Arterburn admits that every man's eyes are naturally drawn to the female form. That's what naturally happens in the moment that a man notices an attractive woman. But in the split-second that it happens, a man can discipline himself to "bounce his eyes" and look away.[9] In Job 31:1, Job admits that, like every other man, there is a temptation to look upon and lust after beautiful women. Thus, he states: *"I made a covenant with my eyes not to look lustfully at a young woman."* If this faithful man had to make a commitment to protect his eyes, then every one of us would be wise to do likewise.

A second discipline for our kids who will be susceptible to lust and temptation is to teach them to pray for those who are caught up in the sex trade. According to most of the people who were once in the porn industry but who have been set free from it, the whole environment is one rampant with abuse, drug use, and exploitation. These people are trapped in a world that is doing significant damage to their hearts and souls. They deserve our mercy and our prayers. Plus, as a friend once told me, it is really hard to lust after someone for whom I am praying.

A third skill to teach our kids is to do what the Bible simply calls "fleeing sexual temptation." We will explore this at length in the next chapter on Scripts, but that Biblical command certainly applies here. In no uncertain terms, we need to tell our kids that if they ever encounter even a hint of sexually explicit content, they need to flee. Run. Get out of there. Remove themselves immediately from the situation. The longer they flirt with it, the harder it will be to disengage from it.

A final recommendation I would make to every parent is that we put parameters on the computers in our homes. If we have children or teens and the family computer does not have some form of filter or blocking software, we are asking for trouble. I will go one step further and call it foolish. We may have complete trust in our kids and we may want them to learn to make wise decisions on their own. Fine. But when I take my preschooler to the pool, I give her clear instructions and expectations for her safety, but I also make her wear a life preserver. Both are important.

With the prevalence of and such easy access to porn on the internet, it is just too risky for our kids to have an instant portal to material that just 25 years ago could only be found in a seedy downtown movie theater.

There are several good products out there, but the technological landscape is constantly changing. A search for "family internet filters" would be a good place to start. XXX Church has a free one. BSecure and Covenant Eyes are also well recommended. Find one that works and get it installed sooner rather than later. The bad news is that a filter might slow down your browser by a little bit. Deal with it.

We can be sure that the marriages of those growing up in this internet generation will be severely impacted by the prevalent use of porn in their developmental years. While we would love to help every young person to avoid becoming entangled in this web of lies, we do not have the power to shut down a profitable, multi-billion dollar industry. Still, may we be parents who do everything we can to minimize its impact on our kids.

eighteen

Scripts

Equipping Our Kids to "Flee Sexual Temptation"

I wonder what it would have been like to be a young man in 1942 in the season when America was aggressively getting into World War II. As someone who is relatively unfamiliar with guns and who doesn't have a violent bone in his body, I wonder how would I have done as a soldier who enlisted in the army? I'm not so sure. I would have definitely needed some help.

Historian Stephen Ambrose has powerfully documented the process of how America transformed millions of average guys like me into the most competent fighting force the world has ever seen. This can be seen in the incredible *Band of Brothers* book and mini-series, but even more clearly in his book, *Citizen Soldiers*. Fitting with the name, Ambrose chronicles how the U.S. military took average American citizens—teachers, accountants, farmers—and turned them into elite and deadly soldiers.

How did they pull it off? Through extensive training.

Ambrose chronicles in great detail the process of preparation that these men endured. Most of the soldiers who successfully stormed the beaches of Normandy had never seen action before that day. But many of them had been training for nearly two years. The military placed its confidence in the tried and true practice of disciplined rehearsal. The hope was that if they trained the men hard enough, their instincts would take over once they got on the battlefield. For the vast majority of these average Joes, it worked.

Imagine what would have happened if they simply gave a 25-year-old factory worker a uniform, put a rifle in his hands, strapped a parachute on his back and said "good luck." What if the first time he jumped out of a plane or fired a gun was when he was being dropped behind enemy lines on D-Day? It would have been disastrous. He would have looked like a soldier, but he certainly wouldn't have had the skills or experience to act like one.

Let's bring this illustration home.

Even if our kids want to do the right thing and have the best of intentions, they will not be successful if we haven't trained them on what to do in a moment of decision. Nancy Reagan's anti-drug strategy of "Just Say No!" is vastly insufficient. It falls well short of what our kids need to do or say.

> *Jenifer's Perspective:*
> *"As parents, how frequently do we do that sort of thing with our kids? We send them into a battlefield full of moral and relational challenges related to their sexuality by saying, 'Make good choices!' That is inadequate to the point of being almost comical."*

The Bible gives us some clear marching orders regarding how each of us is to face the challenges of sexual temptation: *"Flee sexual immorality. All other sins a person commits are outside the body, but whoever sins sexually, sins against their own body."* (1 Corinthians 6:18) The battle plan God gives us is actually no battle plan at all; the plan is to retreat. Flee. Get the heck out of Dodge. God could not be more clear.

If we expect our kids to flee sexual temptation but don't equip them on how to do it, we are failing them. What they need are some

156

"scripts," or clear plans of action of what they will say and do to steer clear of sexual immorality. We can train them in at least three ways:

1. Help Them See the Realities of Temptation

This is probably the hardest sell, because the very thing that Satan is using as a temptation is so attractive in the moment. After all, we don't need to be convinced to flee from something that is clearly dangerous, like a swarm of killer bees or a grizzly bear. In the case of sexual activity, we must help our kids to see that what seems so good will actually be a source of pain and grief.

Consider the warning that Solomon gave in Proverbs 5:3-4: *"For the lips of the adulterous woman drip honey, and her speech is smoother than oil; but in the end she is bitter as gall, sharp as a double-edged sword."*

With their perspective clouded by raging hormones, young people are easily deceived. It is not uncommon for a young person, in a moment of passion, to have a sense that he should flee but not have the desire or strength to do so. Increasing his or her awareness of what is truly going on in the spiritual realm can help. Instead of just saying, "Don't have sex," help them to see that the enemy is deliberately and specifically laying traps to ruin their lives.

2. Help Them Avoid It by Recognizing Warning Signs

Most traditional dating (going out, steady, whatever) is setting our kids up for sexual temptation. We can try to convince ourselves that it's not true, but it is. When our kids are in a relationship, we must realize that we are allowing them to be in circumstances where they are susceptible to hazard.

A part of their equipping should be to help them steer clear of circumstances where they will be likely to be tempted. They should also learn to see the "red flags" of situations that could be troublesome.

1 Samuel 13 tells the tragic story of David's son Amnon and his sick obsession with his sister Tamar. It serves as a cautionary tale and a textbook case of someone who missed all the warning signs. Amnon desperately wanted to have sex with Tamar, so at the

suggestion of one of his advisors, he devised a plan to get her alone. He pretended to be sick and then asked his father David to send Tamar to care for him and make him some homemade bread.

The first person to miss a red flag was David, Tamar's father.

Whether he was too busy to notice Amnon's obsession or he was simply naïve, we do not know. What we do know is that David sent his daughter into a very hazardous situation. (There's a lesson for every dad reading this.)

Tamar went to Amnon's room and made bread right there in his presence. She did just as he requested, but Amnon wouldn't eat it. He suddenly acted like he wasn't interested. There's the second red flag. He said one thing and did another. We must train our kids to become very alert when they find themselves in a situation when someone says one thing but then changes his or her mind.

The third red flag that Tamar should have noticed was when Amnon sent everyone else out of his room, leaving her alone with him. This is clearly significant. We should teach our kids to steer clear of any circumstance where they are home alone with their boyfriend or girlfriend, or in any other isolated place for that matter. Our kids may have the best of intentions, but the potential for temptation is just too great.

A final red flag came when Amnon asked Tamar to sit on his bed and feed him. This was the same guy who just a few minutes ago said he wasn't hungry. In those moments when a discerning teenager senses that something isn't right, it is probably because something isn't right. That troubling sense is most likely the Holy Spirit of God warning them to flee.

3. If They Miss the Signs, Help Them Form a Retreat Plan

The Scriptures give us an encouraging word on this topic, though we are usually not prone to believe it. *"No temptation has overtaken you except what is common to mankind. And God is faithful; he will not let you be tempted beyond what you can bear. But when you are tempted, he will also provide a way out so that you can endure it."* (I Corinthians 10:13) We usually believe that our temptation is too much to handle and we usually believe that there is no way of escape.

158

In Tamar's case, she could have seen some of the red flags, expressed a measure of discomfort with the whole situation, and bolted for the door. Because she didn't, things turned out very badly for her. In fact, once Amnon forced himself on her and robbed her of her innocence, he quickly cast her aside. He was no longer interested. How many young women have experienced that very thing? These are the truths about fleeing sexual temptation that we must begin to engrain in our kids long before we think we need to.

Temptation is a Slippery Slope

Several years ago, I had the chance to take a mission trip to Zambia, Africa. After a full week of ministry, we concluded our time with a road trip to Victoria Falls.

With a width of more than a mile, the falls were like nothing I had ever seen before. While the rest of my group chose to see the falls from a safely distant observation platform, I wanted to get closer. I rented some rain gear (because the water flow is like being in a thunderstorm) and walked over to get a closer look.

I finally got to a place where I could see the falls in all their spectacular glory. Carrying my camera in a plastic bag to keep it dry, I pulled it out to take a few pictures, but the angle from the trail I was on wasn't quite right. With no one to tell me not to, I climbed over the fence that marked the trail and climbed down a steep slope towards the Zambezi River, hoping to get a better look at the falls. Finally, hanging over the side of a cliff I had the perfect view. I took a few pictures, feeling quite proud of myself. Then I looked around. I realized that I was alone, wearing rented flip flops, and standing on a steep, muddy slope with the river some 200 feet below me. One little slip climbing back up to the trail and I would tumble to my death. They would never find my body and nobody would ever know what happened to me. This realization inspired me to climb back up the hill with extreme care.

While I was still far above the river, the slippery slope I was standing on had the unique power to take my life. Our kids must learn that sexual immorality is just like that slippery slope. While they might feel like they are far removed from significant sexual sin,

159

one false move and they will find themselves in a situation where they are certainly over their heads.

Few Christ-followers who find themselves outside of God's will in regards to their sexuality end up there because they deliberately chose to be. What happens more frequently is that they took baby steps down a slippery slope and suddenly found themselves in a situation where they felt powerless to turn back. They didn't mean to fall, but still they fell. What they need most is a heart for God that compels them to stay on the trail and avoid any semblance of sexual sin. This is why God tells us to flee.

Obviously, the last thing the parent of an elementary-aged child wants to do is to coach their kids on what it looks like to steer clear of sexual sin. We don't want to introduce issues that are many years removed from their lives. However, the same thing that brought success to our citizen soldiers can prove helpful to our kids: the more advanced training we can give them, the better prepared they will be for the challenges they will face.

For this reason alone, parents will do well to define as early as possible exactly what sexual immorality is. In a post-Lewinski world where even the President of the United States has a hard time articulating what sex is, we must call our kids to a standard of radical purity. We must encourage our kids to save any and all sexual activity for marriage.

Every teenager in a romantic relationship will seek to know the answer to the age-old question of "how far is too far?" What they are essentially asking is, "How close can I get to the line of sin without actually crossing over it?" Wise parents of younger children will seek to make that question irrelevant by replacing it with a better question: "How holy can I become?" Instead of seeing how close they can get to the line, it is far better to train our kids to have a heart that is set upon pleasing God in all things. This is a concept that even the youngest child can begin to embrace. If our teenagers must have a line not to cross, I would venture to say that God's ideals are a bit more rigorous than ours. Isn't that usually the case?

I can remember a discussion on this years ago in a seminary class. A young single student gave this very stoic advice: "Passionate kissing is fine, just so long as the genitals are not involved." As a newlywed man, I had to disagree. I quickly chimed in: "If the kissing is any good, the genitals will be involved." Uncomfortable laughter followed. My point was that it is impossible for two people to make out for 10 minutes and not become sexually aroused. That's the whole point of making out. If your goal isn't sexual arousal, it would be best to skip it altogether. That's like taking pictures on the edge of a slippery, muddy hill above a 200-foot drop and hoping for the best.

Sooner rather than later, we should paint a picture for our kids of a young single life that is free of sexual activity. We should encourage them to save all their moments of intimacy for their spouse. Most importantly, we should help provide them with what to do and say (scripts) to successfully flee sexual temptation.

How to Talk About Scripts

The basic goal of coaching on scripts is for our kids to be prepared to do the right thing when they encounter a tempting situation. Giving them the responsibility (and eventually trust) for decision-making is an essential part of our parenting. Parenting guru Kim John Payne put it this way: "Independence isn't doing your own thing; it's doing the right thing on your own."

The simplest way to describe this process is as role-playing. You describe some of the situations in which your kids are likely to find themselves. Then you help them to think about what they might say to get out of the situation. It is best if you start doing this long before they are likely to encounter the scenario. You need to talk about fleeing sexual temptation long before your daughter is walking out the door with her prom date. You need to talk about porn long before your son is 15 years old. Here are a few suggested role-plays and scripts:

Situation for elementary aged kids: You are on the school bus and somebody shows you a picture or video on their phone of someone with their clothes off.

Possible Script: *"That's not for me."* Coach him to immediately look or move away from the situation.

Situation for teen daughters: The boy you like puts his hands on your breast/rear/genitals.

Possible Script: (After clearly backing away.) *"No. You don't have my permission to go there. I'm not going to discuss this. How you respond right now will determine the future of our relationship."*

Situation for teen boys: The girl you like is being physically/sexually aggressive.

Possible Script: *"I don't want to take advantage of you like that. I want to guard and protect you, even from me. I want to honor you enough not to take something that isn't mine to take."*

Situation for teens of both genders: You find yourself in a house alone with your boyfriend/girlfriend.

Possible Script: *"It's not wise for us to be here. If you have to grab something inside, I will wait for you in the car."*

Situation for any young person: Somebody offers you alcohol or drugs at a party.

Possible Script: *"I'm not interested. Alcohol makes me stupid and I don't feel like being stupid tonight."*

Beyond simple scripts, it is wise to help our kids to develop some clearly defined standards in some of these areas. These standards aren't meant to be legalistic, but only serve as guardrails similar to those that I climbed over on the path overlooking Victoria Falls. They are there to help us to avoid the slippery slope that is sexual temptation. They will also help our kids to determine if the people they date value the same things that they value. Here are a few rules that you might want to establish for your kids early on:

- Absolutely no kissing of any kind when in a private place.
- Don't be alone at someone's house.
- If you are at a party where there is alcohol or drugs, you need to leave.
- Regarding physical contact, don't do anything that you wouldn't do if Jesus were right there with you (because He is).

- I even heard someone suggest that girls not shave their legs when they are with their boyfriends. Not a bad idea.

The key here is to encourage our kids to avoid situations where they are likely to stumble, because our hearts are prone to sin. Pastor and author Matt Chandler describes it this way: "Put a plate of chips and salsa in front of me and eventually I'm going to eat them."

We must lead our kids to understand that there is a war on for their hearts and minds. Their enemy is extraordinarily sneaky and crafty. His strategy is to take the very thing that will destroy their lives and dress it up in a way that they think they can't live without it. In 1 Peter 5:8 we are called to *"be alert and of sober mind"* because our enemy *"prowls around like a roaring lion looking for someone to devour."*

Regarding our kids, there is no battlefield that he is more aggressive on than in this area of sexual temptation. Since those battle lines have been drawn, may we be parents who give our kids the tools and training to fight back and be successful in the battle. May we help our kids to walk with the God who will supernaturally empower them to stand strong when they face temptation.

nineteen

Marriage

Laying out a Potential Path for Our Kids

I have a great deal of empathy for parents reading this who might feel a bit overwhelmed with what seems like a long list of conversations they need to have with their kids. The typical parent might have a gnawing question developing in his gut: "If we are teaching our kids these principles, engaging them in meaningful conversation about relationships, and guarding them from giving their heart away too soon, how will they ever get married?" This is a great question.

Early on, parents need to lay out a potential path that their kids might walk when they feel God is leading them to a spouse. I am not suggesting a legalistic, one-size-fits-all approach. I am simply offering an alternative to what we typically see in our world; a system that suggests we "try on different people until we find the perfect fit." Instead, I want to describe a possible scenario for our kids that I have experienced first-hand.

As I write these words, I am still basking in the joy of the recent wedding of my oldest daughter. On the day of her wedding, Lindsey was 19 and her husband, Christian, was 20. Yes, I know. They married young. However, the story I saw God tell through their lives was absolutely amazing. While the path they took to get married was not typical, it serves as a God-honoring alternative to what our culture has embraced as normal. Unfortunately, what is normal is not working. With the average age for marriage in America at almost 27 for women and 29 for men, there are some serious flaws in our system. With that in mind, I want to attempt to make a case for young marriage.

Our culture is wary of "early marriage," convinced that the younger a couple marries, the greater the likelihood that their marriage will fail. In reality, that's only true for those who marry in their teens. According to a 2002 study by the Centers for Disease Control, those who marry in their teens do, in fact, have a relatively high chance of their marriage failing. The divorce rate is 48% for those who marry under 18 years of age and 40% for those who are 18-19.

However, for those who marry between the ages of 20-24, the divorce rate drops to 29%, similar to the 24% of the 25 years and older group.[1] There is no strong statistical evidence to suggest that delaying marriage until our kids have their lives completely in order (their late 20's, for example) will help them to be more successful. I'm not even sure how our culture almost unanimously came to that conclusion, especially in light of history.

> *Jenifer's Perspective:*
> *"My grandparents married when he was 18 and she was 16. It was a different world then, but they had stability and longevity that few marriages today ever experience."*

Consider our grandparents' generation: what we now refer to as the "Greatest Generation." It was commonplace for those born in the first thirty years of the last century to marry at about 20 years old, raise a large family, and stay married for sixty years. For the most part, they lived out their commitment in a way that left a legacy of strength and security to the generations that followed them. They may not have been perfectly happy every moment, but they endured, experiencing a measure of peace and joy that no generation has known since.

Contrast that with our thinking today. Many parents have become so enlightened with the belief that the best thing they can possibly do for their kids is force them to have their life entirely in order before they marry. Most wouldn't dream of allowing their kids to walk the aisle until they have sufficiently jumped through some non-negotiable hoops. For example, parents require their kids to finish college, get a job, and have everything in life lined up (noble goals every one). What they don't realize is that they are inadvertently prioritizing financial security over personal holiness.

Here's a news flash: young adults are wired to have sex. The great hypocrisy among Christian parents is that we encourage abstinence in our kids, yet we push our kids to have everything figured out before they marry. This is a toxic combination: don't have sex...but don't get married.

The truth is that God wants young adults to exercise their sexuality, but only in the context of marriage. The problem in our culture is that we put marriage off too long. The inevitable result is that many young people end up feeling broken and alone due to the guilt of making poor choices regarding their sexuality. In our current system we are setting them up for failure and a sense of defeat.

Renowned sociologist Mark Regnerus describes how Christian young adults have come to think: "They would rather deal with sexual guilt—if they sense any at all—than consider marrying before they think they are ready." Thankfully, he also offers a solution to Christian parents: "This cultural predilection toward punishing rather than blessing marriage must go, and congregations and churchgoers can help by dropping their own punitive positions toward family members."[2]

The Scriptures address this very thing in 1 Corinthians 7:9 *"If they cannot control themselves, they should marry, for it is better to marry than to burn with passion."* Parents must be willing to remove obstacles for their kids so that when God leads them to the person they want to commit to in marriage, they are ready. We must take an honest look at the path we are laying out for our kids.

There is nothing wrong with encouraging our kids to finish college before they marry, but we must not see that as a non-negotiable requirement. If we are willing to support them financially as a single college student, why wouldn't we support them as a married college student? A friend of mine jokes that they will probably make better grades that way because they won't be thinking about sex all the time.

What might be needed is a broader shift in our philosophy. Instead of spending all our time telling them "don't do it," parents should focus our energies on preparing them for adulthood. This way, they can experience all that God designed them to be as adults: emotionally, relationally, spiritually, AND sexually. If a parent feels that his young adult is not ready for marriage, maybe their goal should be to proactively help them to get ready, not to empower them for a prolonged adolescence.

In his book, *Emerging Adulthood,* Jeffrey Jensen Arnett writes: "Many of the identity explorations of the emerging adult years are simply for fun, a kind of play, part of gaining a broad range of life experiences before 'settling down' and taking on the responsibilities of adult life."[3] It is as if we are encouraging our kids to practice being selfish as opposed to learning how to love another person well. Four years of self-focused freedom in college may seem like a good thing, but it is counterproductive to where most of our kids will eventually find themselves: sharing a life and a home with another in a covenant marriage.

We must present this goal of marriage as one to be desired and one that can be achieved. Instead of insisting that our kids put if off indefinitely, we should prayerfully consider how we can prepare them for life with a marriage partner.

In 2009, Regnerus wrote in *Christianity Today* that "the message must change, because our preoccupation with sex has unwittingly turned our attention away from the damage that Americans—including evangelicals—are doing to the institution of marriage by discouraging and delaying it." He concluded, "Christians have made much ado about sex but are becoming slow and lax about marriage."[4]

Instead of focusing all our attention on "don't have sex," as parents we should start preparing our children for the responsibilities of marriage even while they are teenagers. We should be diligent to teach our sons how to step up into noble manhood and our daughters how to be Godly wives. We should coach them on having the right kind of marriage, being the right kind of person, becoming financially independent, and being prepared to commit to another person free from a lot of baggage. There will be some baggage, no doubt, but we should help our kids to minimize it in every way we can.

Over the past eight years, Jenifer and I have counseled more than 500 engaged couples through a series of Marriage Prep workshops. I have concluded that all newlywed couples have challenges, regardless of their age. The really young couples struggle with financial security and a measure of childlike innocence that, early on, cause them to stumble through some of the big issues of life.

In contrast, those marrying in their late 20's or early 30's have a different set of problems. They realize the challenge of making decisions for two when they have spent ten plus years of their adult lives considering only themselves. They also typically have the relational byproducts that come from a decade of dating and playing the field.

If I had to choose which problems to enter marriage with, I would choose the childlike innocence any day. At the very least, these young couples get to stumble through life with the love of their lives close beside them.

How to Talk About Marriage

When giving a prescription for marriage, the Bible articulates on four different occasions that we are to leave our father and mother and cleave to our spouse. Genesis 2:24, Matthew 19:5, Mark 10:7 and Ephesians 5:31 all use this language. The word "cleave" is found in the King James and I like it, not only because it conveniently rhymes with leave (and is perfect for sermon material), but also because it suggests a powerful, inseparable bond. If these two words are fundamental to God's design for marriage, we would do well to talk to our kids about them as such.

1. Get Ready to "Leave"

Young people have no right to cleave to another person until they are prepared to leave their father and mother's house. This is a
168

Biblical principle that most young people have totally ignored, connecting (in varying degrees of commitment) to numerous people before they come anywhere close to leaving their dependence on mom and dad. Preparing to leave means becoming emotionally, spiritually, and relationally independent so a person can fully commit to a spouse.

The parents of my son-in-law did this better than just about anybody I have ever seen. From a very early age, they told their son the truth from Proverbs 24:27: *"Put your outdoor work in order and get your fields ready; after that, build your house."*

Essentially, they told him that he couldn't pursue a wife (or even a girlfriend) until he was prepared to leave his home. This motivated him to become a man, instead of wallowing around in the carefree life of the typical adolescent. I'm not suggesting that every 18-year-old needs to have a career and be fully independent of his parents, but we must begin to intentionally train our kids to prepare to leave.

Will their character be fully developed or will they be completely mature? Probably not. But instead of seeing marriage as the thing they do once they have their entire lives in order, why not help our kids to make a priority of growing up and preparing to leave home? Once God leads them to the person they are willing to commit to, they can grow up and mature fully alongside that person. Mark Regnerus puts it this way: "Most young Americans no longer think of marriage as a formative institution, but rather as the institution they enter once they think they are fully formed."[5]

> *Jenifer's Perspective:*
> *"Nothing will form a person's character like*
> *marriage. We all know this to be true."*

As for the issue of financial independence, there is nothing inherently wrong with desiring our kids to be financially on their own before they marry. Many parents have made it difficult for their kids to "leave" because they seek to control their kids' lives with money and other forms of support. However, I am not sure of the wisdom of allowing the money dimension to trump all the other challenges facing a young couple in love. Our goal should be to help and affirm any young couple that is obviously striving for Godliness and Christian fidelity.

2. Save The "Cleave"

Depending on the depth of any relationship, the potential for creating "soul ties" is always there. In certain non-romantic relationships, powerful bonds are often formed in highly emotional circumstances: serving on the battlefield of war or suffering through a common trial can significantly knit two people together. In opposite-sex relationships, soul ties can also be formed by emotional, spiritual, and sexual closeness. Seemingly innocent friendships with the opposite-sex can quickly blossom into a romantic connection, often without notice.

This is why it is important that we coach our kids not to "cleave" too quickly with someone else. If they share their deepest emotional thoughts and feelings with every person they have even the potential for a romantic relationship with, they will often find that they develop a soul tie that will last through much of life. Ultimately, they will look back from marriage and realize that they gave something away to someone who was not their spouse. I'm not referring just to sex. There is value in teaching our kids to save themselves for marriage emotionally just as they are saving themselves physically.

This is yet another reason I have found myself to be an advocate for young marriage. The longer a person lives, the more they will desire to give their heart away to another person. If they are not careful, they can end up giving pieces of their hearts away to so many people that it is difficult to fully give it to the one they eventually marry. The good news of the cross is that Christ can fully restore a person's heart. However, we all know that this person is likely to spend a lifetime learning how to fully receive God's restoration. A far better option is to keep the heart as intact as possible until we are able to fully cleave to another.

3. Stop Looking for a "Soul Mate"

Did God create a person for each one of us to marry? Perhaps. In His sovereign will, I assume He knows who each person will choose, for better or for worse. But that's God's business to know, not ours. If we suggest to our kids that they have to find their perfect mate, the one that God pre-ordained for them to marry, then they are likely to drive themselves crazy with the pressure of not messing it up.

Instead of some shallow romantic sense that they have found their "soul mate," parents should teach some key non-negotiables on who they should ultimately marry. As your son or daughter enters the stage of life where marriage is becoming a possibility and a potential spouse meets the criteria, then they can begin to prayerfully consider if they are willing to commit themselves to the person. Some things they can look for include:

- He is a committed believer.
- His inner character is moving toward Christlikeness.
- Both have the blessing and affirmation of their parents and/or other Godly people in their lives.
- The relationship is free of any significant incompatibilities.
- They are nearing a life stage where they are both ready to leave and cleave. (Emotionally, relationally, and practically.)

These are the marks of a marry-able person. They are far more critical yet more attainable than the esoteric goal of finding "the one." If one of my kids has become a young adult and can affirm these things in the person they are "in love with" (and the feeling is mutual), then it might be time to start planning a wedding. This could be true even if they are still shy of their 20th birthday.

4. Move Ahead in Faith

When we consider the maturity of the average twenty-year-old, the outlook is not particularly encouraging. Young adults from this generation can be markedly immature, self-serving, and unprepared for the challenges of life as a grownup. Encouraging them to get married may seem like the most foolhardy action imaginable.

Instead of embracing this paradigm as the unchangeable status quo, we should envision a different path for our kids. Yes, the vast majority of young people might be characterized by immaturity, but it does not have to describe *our* kids. (In fact, there are whole populations of young adults today who are more selfless and Christ-focused than any generation before them.) We just have to be intentional in preparing them for adulthood and marriage.

When my son-in-law Christian came to me as an 18-year-old college sophomore and told me he wanted to marry my daughter (and soon), I responded with, "Let's talk about that." I was willing to give it serious consideration because I knew that his parents had been preparing him for that very thing. They had encouraged him to prepare his heart, to save his money, and to allow God to shape his character. I also knew that my Lindsey had been allowing God to do the exact same things in her life.

Six months later, Christian proposed to Lindsey at the edge of a lake in a private moment at a family gathering in Texas. A year after that, they pledged themselves to one another before God as well as 450 friends and family in what was without a doubt the most beautiful and Spirit-filled wedding I have ever experienced. Their busy first year of marriage has included college for both of them, a part-time engineering job for Christian, and the recent birth of a baby conceived in the first few weeks of marriage. Has it been challenging? Of course it has, but certainly no more difficult than what every newlywed couple experiences. In the end, God has been gracious to them and Christian and Lindsey would say that they are having the time of their lives.

These early days of barely making it financially and trusting in God for everything has done far more to build strength in their marriage than having every aspect of their lives in order ever could have done. They are laying a foundation and building memories similar to what their great-grandparents from the "Greatest Generation" experienced. I am thankful for the legacy of commitment and faithfulness that my ancestors left for them. I am also extremely hopeful for the legacy that my kids will leave to the generations that follow them.

As Christian parents, may we not allow the world's value system to dictate to us the pathway our kids must take towards marriage. May we come to place a greater value on holiness than we do on the world's idea of security. Finally, may we look to God for help as we prepare our kids for both the challenges and joys of married life.

twenty

Abuse

Keeping Our Kids from Harm

I seriously considered bypassing the topic of sexual abuse and trauma altogether, as it is so distasteful and uncomfortable. However, there is a relatively high likelihood that someone is going to try to take advantage of our kids at some point. Failing to equip them for that possibility is a significant failure on our part.

Sex is hard enough to talk to our innocent children about, much less having to deal with the horrifying possibility that someone could potentially overpower and violate them. If we have done a poor job of discussing sex with our kids, it is likely we have lived in a fog of denial about the realities of child sexual abuse. Because of our discomfort, our kids may have been left vulnerable.

The statistics are hard to quantify (because so much abuse goes unreported), but we can be sure that incidences of child sexual abuse are on the rise. Beyond the fact that it is widespread, the personal trauma of abuse is also a heavy burden for a child to bear alone. Victims of child sexual abuse are often shamed into silence, afraid of the repercussions of disclosure, and unfortunately, their parents are usually the last to know.

Why do our children suffer in silence? We trust those closest to us—our family, friends, coaches and teachers—so it is most difficult to accept that the vast majority of abusers are people that the victim knows and trusts. The abuser often carries credibility in the parent's life, so the child feels not only shame but also that they won't be believed.

For a clearer understanding of the issue, consider how the Centers for Disease Control define child sexual abuse:

Child sexual abuse involves any sexual activity with a child where consent is not or cannot be given. This includes sexual contact that is accompanied by force or threat, regardless of age to participants, and all sexual contact between an adult and a child, regardless of whether or not there is deception or the child understands the sexual nature of the activity. Sexual contact between an older and younger child can also be abusive if there is significant disparity in age, development, or size, rendering the younger child incapable of giving informed consent. The sexual abuse acts may include sexual penetration, sexual touching, or non-contact sexual acts such as voyeurism or exhibitionism.[1]

Recognize that this definition is quite broad and that it includes a plethora of abuses that fall far short of actual penetration. Just because a situation of abuse is not as extreme as that, we should not discount its impact as insignificant, as all types of abuse have the potential to negatively impact our kids' perceptions of their God-given sexuality.

A Perpetrator's Strategy

Perpetrators are cunning, manipulative and very patient to target their prey. They use a process called "grooming" to test the vulnerability of a child, building trust with the child and slowly preparing to overcome that child with sexual power. Grooming happens in a number of ways. They may show the child extra attention or affirmation. The abuser may tickle, they may cuddle, wrestle, kiss or find other ways to make physical contact with the child. The inappropriate touch or action may appear as an accident. If the child says nothing, the second try may be followed by, "You liked it when I did that yesterday, let me try it again and show you how good it feels," leaving the child confused, embarrassed and ashamed.

Children are most vulnerable when they are going through transition (family illness, death in the family, move, divorce), when they need affirmation, attention, and when they are ill-prepared to respond to the risk of sexual abuse. Some children are made to feel consensual in the act and may become paralyzed with fear. The perpetrator convinces the child that this is their secret, never to be told. Children are groomed by fear and intimidation and hear phrases like: "No one will believe you. If you tell I'll hurt you, your mother, or your sister. If you tell I'll put these pictures on the internet for everyone to see. If you tell you will be in a lot of trouble for what you have done."

We may be confident that our children are smart and that they would not fall prey to this type of "grooming." Or we might believe that our children would tell us if someone makes them feel uncomfortable or touches them inappropriately. Still, if we do not prepare and equip them for these possibilities, it is likely that a perpetrator will gain the upper hand of influence, using shame and fear to deceive our kids into silence.

It is also critical that parents be aware of the signs of sexual abuse in children. If we can know what to look for, we will be best prepared to address any type of abuse before it has a chance to create a significant impact on the lives of our kids.

What are some signs of sexual abuse? First and foremost, know that there may be no signs at all. However, what we want to be on the lookout for is a drastic change in behavior that we cannot explain. Consider a few of the components found on a list compiled by The Child Molestation Research and Prevention Institute.

Signs a Child is Being Abused

• Touching genitals of others or inducing fear or threats of force.

175

- Sexually explicit conversations with significant age difference.
- Repeated peeping, exposing, obscenities, or pornographic interest.
- Oral, vaginal, anal penetration of dolls, other children, or animals.
- Any genital injury or bleeding not explained by accidental cause.
- Preoccupation with sexual play.
- Forcing any sexual activity on others.
- Engaging in sexually explicit conversations.[2]

Parents would also be wise to be on the lookout for dramatic changes in their child or teen's behavior. They should not dismiss their child's isolation or withdrawal as simply evidence of puberty or hormonal surges. While that may be the case, seeing one or more of these signs would be worth some measure of inquiry. Witnessing a dramatic change in behavior should at least bring a parent to give closer attention to the child's interactions with older youth or adults. Does the child seem uncomfortable around certain people, even frightened or embarrassed? If so, then a warm, loving, and safe conversation with a few specific questions might be in order.

Some questions or statements a concerned parent might ask would include:

- Is everything okay with _____?
- Has anything happened between you and _____?
- Sometimes a person might make you feel uncomfortable or even hurt you, and then warn you that you can't tell anyone. Know that any person who says that cannot be trusted.
- You know that you can tell me anything and I won't be mad.
- I'm here to help you and keep you safe. If you don't feel safe with someone, it is okay for you to tell me about it.

Parents must realize that their children are looking to them for protection. Any steps parents take to intervene will promote justice, hope and healing. If some form of abuse is discovered, know that it will require great courage to act decisively on behalf of the child.

176

Parents must do the right thing by reporting the abuser to the appropriate authorities.

How to Talk About Abuse

The sooner parents can give their kids a voice regarding sexual abuse, the better. Parents must help them understand that there is power in their voice and that no one can take that power away from them. We have to take responsibility to teach our children about the possibility of sexual abuse. More importantly, we must teach them to respect their bodies and the bodies of others. Our kids' ages will dictate what and when we might share with them.

Talking with Preschoolers

We must realize that abuse can happen to even the youngest of children, so we must start our strategy of prevention when our kids are very young. This can be as simple as explaining at bath time which parts of the body are private and should never be touched by another adult or child. Pointing out those parts that are always covered by their bathing suit is a good rule of thumb. Let your child know that if anyone touches them in these private areas they must come and tell you—no matter who it is.

Talking with Children

Perhaps the best thing a parent can do during the developmental childhood years is to be a good listener. Always be open and available and listen carefully to what the child's natural curiosities are. When it comes time to address issues of abuse, a wise parent will already be aware of what their kids are aware of. Do not try to cover every detail at once, but plan a specific time to sit down and discuss this topic. Keep the language simple but always use correct terms. If the child has a basic awareness of sexual intercourse, then hopefully they grasp that all aspects of sexuality (including all their private parts) are reserved for adults in marriage. This knowledge will enable the parent to coach their kids to be on the lookout for anyone who is trying to take advantage of them. If nothing else, this makes a solid argument for starting sex education at an earlier age than we are typically comfortable with.

Talking with Teenagers

For some reason, parents become reluctant to talk about the specifics of sexual behavior and activity once their kids become teenagers. We have had numerous occasions when our teenagers' friends have asked us pretty explicit questions at our house, all because their parents refuse to talk about it at their house. Which begs the question: "Is there such a thing as giving too much information?" The answer is "No." Information does not encourage a child to be sexually active.

What teenagers need is help to navigate these waters and even coaching to be on the lookout for abuses by others. I have personally heard of enough cases of "date rape" happening to innocent girls that I barely want to let my teenagers out of my sight. Our daughters need to have a sense of empowerment in their minds that will enable them to get out of "red flag" situations like I mentioned in the chapter on Scripts.

Our teenagers definitely need to know about date rape drugs. While the most popular one is Rohypnol (Roofies), other drugs commonly used include GHB, Ketamine, and even Ambien. They need to know how these are used and that even charming and good-looking young men will try to slip them into their drinks at parties. One specific lesson we must teach our teenage girls (and even our boys): "At a party, do not EVER take a drink that someone gives you. Ever."

Beyond the drugs that are used by men to take advantage of women, we must coach our kids that recreational drugs and alcohol can quickly make them targets of sexual abuse. A few headline-grabbing trials in recent days have showed us that foolish and energetic young men have the real potential to take advantage of young women who are not fully sober.

The most powerful tools we can give our children are education, clear personal boundaries, and personal power. These are a lifetime of lessons, often practiced in the most risky of situations. Most importantly, our children need to know that we love them and that

178

we will always believe them and support them in any case of sexual abuse. They also need to know that we will fight for justice, no matter the identity of the abuser. Child sexual abuse is a crime that takes great courage to face and greater courage to report. We must be parents of great courage.

It goes without saying that these issues are uncomfortable. They can make any parent feel afraid and overwhelmed. While this brief chapter only skimmed the surface, there are many resources available for parents who want to become better equipped in guarding and protecting their kids. One such resource is my friend Angela Williams of VOICE Today. She has personally experienced both the pain of sexual trauma and the amazing restoration that can only be found at the cross. I encourage you to learn more about her story and ministry at www.voicetoday.org.

If you need some specific help or guidance on these issues, please aggressively and quickly seek out a trusted counselor with wisdom and experience in this area. Just as no innocent child should have to face this alone, no family should feel like they are alone in seeking help and healing from sexual trauma. Get help. It is out there.

Part Three:
Becoming the Parent Your
Kids Desperately Need

twenty-one

Influence

There are no shortcuts.
You must connect with your child's heart.

"Son, we need to talk."

That is how a parent might be tempted to begin a dialogue with his child or teenager about the issues we have kicked around in this book. However, if there isn't a meaningful love relationship between the parent and his child, then it is probably not going to go very well. The tension will only increase if the parent starts placing a bunch of new rules and guidelines on his son. If he doesn't have his son's heart and there isn't a lot of trust between the two, then it's probably not going to go very well.

I have heard Josh McDowell say, "Rules without relationship will lead to rebellion." I think he is right. As a parent, if I put a bunch of rigid rules on how my daughter interacts with boys and I do not have her heart, I should prepare myself for World War III. However, as a general rule, if I have stayed diligent to gain and maintain her heart, she may not always like the parameters I set, but she is far more likely to submit to them.

Much has been said about parents being parents and not their children's friends. Experts agree that one of the biggest mistakes parents can make is striving too hard to be their child's buddy. The result for some has been an extreme swing in the wrong direction: parents who actually make it their goal to remain emotionally disconnected from their children. As one father I heard put it: "My goal with my teenagers is to make sure they don't like me." I think he is missing the point.

Jenifer and I sat in a conference with Stuart and Jill Briscoe a few years ago. This amazing couple, who have both long since passed their 70th year, had much to say about the lessons they have learned through the years about parenting. I clearly remember Jill casually stressing the importance of the connection between a parent and child: "You want them to like you. If they don't like you, they won't listen to you. After all, do you listen to people that you don't like?"

> Jenifer's Perspective:
> "If anyone is being stirred by God to develop a plan for addressing these relational and sexual issues with their kids, then the place to start is in the parent/child relationship. We must have our children's hearts!"

Many parents will be convicted by something in this book and start looking for the immediate safeguards they can put around their kids to protect them. This is a classic case of putting the cart before the horse. Consider what Brenda Hunter says in her book on middle school life, *From Santa to Sexting*:

> In our quest to keep our children safe, have we settled for smoke and mirrors? Have we put our faith in things, not relationships? Have things, over the years, become a substitute for on-site parental supervision and presence? As parents, we plan for virtually every exigency:
> Antibacterial lotion? Check.
> Kids who know to stop, drop, and roll if they're on fire? Check.
> Kids who run from strangers? Check.
> Charged-up cell phone to receive our incessant texts? Check.

Many of our children have every gadget known to man. But do they have us? Do they own our hearts? Our time? In short, do they have warm, secure, stable connections with us?[1]

The very last verse in the Old Testament is Malachi 4:6. It gives a prophecy about the ministry of a new Elijah who will *"turn the hearts of the parents to their children, and the hearts of the children to their parents. . . ."* When all has been said and done in the old covenant, this is the final word that God gives us.

After four hundred years of silence, at the very beginning of the New Testament, we see another reference to this new Elijah (who we learn is John the Baptist). There in Luke 1:17, it similarly says that he will *"turn the hearts of the parents to their children and the disobedient to the wisdom of the righteous—to make ready a people prepared for the Lord."*

The Old Testament ends with this theme and the New Testament opens with it. What is evident is that one element critical to the ushering in of the Kingdom of God is the heart connection between parent and child. This love relationship is the primary means by which our faith is passed from one generation to the next. When the love relationship is severed or broken, our ability to influence the next generation is limited. When it is nurtured to be strong, our influence is great. While that principle is true for issues of faith, it is true for any other value we want to teach our children, as well.

Sadly, many parents have bought the lie that their influence is minimal when compared with their child's peers, particularly on the issue of sex and relationships. So they sit passively by, waiting for their child to come to them asking for advice or insight, when in fact, the truth remains that parents are still the most powerful influence on their kids. Furthermore, most kids (including teenagers) are desperately wanting their parents to speak wisdom into their lives.

Consider what some current research tells us:

Anheuser-Busch did a study in 2012 about who influences teenagers the most. With regards to an issue like drinking alcohol, the researchers were surprised to learn that parents were the number one influence on 73% of teenagers. In contrast, best friends were listed as the number one influence by only 8% of teens.[2] They found that parental influence was maximized when it was leveraged through healthy relationships with their children.

According to a 2012 study by the National Campaign to Prevent Teen Pregnancy, when teens were asked about who is most influential about their personal decisions about sex, 87% believe it would be easier for teens to postpone sexual activity and avoid teen pregnancy if they were able to have more open, honest conversations about these topics with their parents.[3]

In that same study, when asked who influences teens most in dating relationships, 35% said it was their parents. Friends came in at 28%. Religious leaders were only 3%.[4] This speaks volumes about the relative influence of parents and youth leaders. We cannot assume that our kids are getting the right message just because we take them to church.

How Do We Get Our Children's Hearts?

We can be certain that there are no shortcuts to capturing our kids' hearts and fostering a love relationship with them. It will take time, energy and a significant movement of God. We should start by asking God to do what only He can do: supernaturally turn our hearts back to the hearts of our children.

This is not easy. In those times when my energy is spent, my focus is gone, and my kids are getting what can only be described as the "leftovers" of my life, I need God to turn my heart back to my children. This starts with me asking Him to move and then giving Him access to my life to do so. If I fail to regularly put myself in this position of humility, I am apt to be content spending my evenings watching TV instead of connecting in a meaningful way with my kids.

What must parents do to capture the hearts of their children? How can parents keep their hearts once they have them? There is an excellent example of this very thing in the life of Absalom, the son of King David. The Bible says that he successfully *"stole the hearts of the people of Israel,"* shifting the allegiance of the people from his father to himself and enabling him to step in as king. While our desire is not to overthrow a government, but to maintain a prominent place of love and influence in our kids' lives, we can learn from Absalom.

186

How did Absalom gain the hearts of the people? The first six verses of 1 Samuel 15 tell the story:

"In the course of time, Absalom provided himself with a chariot and horses and with fifty men to run ahead of him. He would get up early and stand by the side of the road leading to the city gate. Whenever anyone came with a complaint to be placed before the king for a decision, Absalom would call out to him, "What town are you from?" He would answer, "Your servant is from one of the tribes of Israel." Then Absalom would say to him, "Look, your claims are valid and proper, but there is no representative of the king to hear you." And Absalom would add, "If only I were appointed judge in the land! Then everyone who has a complaint or case could come to me and I would see that they receive justice." Also, whenever anyone approached him to bow down before him, Absalom would reach out his hand, take hold of him and kiss him. Absalom behaved in this way toward all the Israelites who came to the king asking for justice, and so he stole the hearts of the people of Israel."

There are five things that parents can learn from Absalom's actions. They are, in many ways, obvious dimensions of parenting that should be evident in our homes on a daily basis. If you feel that you don't "have your child's heart," then it is likely that you have neglected these things in recent days.

1. We Must Invest Significant Time in the Relationship

The first part of verse two says that Absalom *"would get up early and stand by the side of road leading to the city gate."* He went out of his way to be where he was likely to come into contact with the people. Getting up early was a sacrifice of his time, but he knew it was worth it.

In a similar way, parents must carve time out of their busy schedules to be with their kids. My friend Tommy had a great relationship with his daughter when she was a teenager. I would ask him what he did and his answer was always "cards." She liked to play cards. He discovered that when he would sit at the table for a few hours and play cards, they would slowly develop a heart connection and she would eventually open up about what was going on in her life.

As it relates to the specific issue of sexual behavior in teens, the time a family spends together is critical for a teen to develop healthy habits. A study published in *Child Development* in 2009 found that family activities were the most important protective factor against teen sex. Teens who ate dinner with their families and engaged in other types of family activities on a regular basis had lower sexual risk behaviors than the average teenager.[5]

While the next four things that Absalom did are skills that can be learned, this first one may require some radical adjustments to our lives, but it is essential if we truly want to have our kids' hearts.

2. We Must Take an Interest in Their World

The second part of verse two describes how Absalom took a sincere interest in what was troubling the people of Israel. *"Whenever anyone came with a complaint to be placed before the king for a decision, Absalom would call out to him, 'What town are you from?' He would answer, 'Your servant is from one of the tribes of Israel.'"*

In effect, Absalom did what peer groups prone to unhealthy behaviors have been doing for teens for generations. Most teenagers who pull away from the positive influence of home and become significantly influenced in a negative way by a peer group will say basically the same thing: "My parents don't listen to me; my friends do." When a teen feels that he is not valued or that his opinion and perspective don't matter in the home, why wouldn't he pull away?

Just like Absalom did, we must learn to ask questions of our kids and then take time to listen to their answers, not with preconceived notions of what they will say, and not with a plan to make sure we have the final word when the conversation ends. We need to ask questions and then shut up and listen. It may take a while to get past the initial grunts and short answers that teenagers are prone to give. If we are first investing time and then truly taking an interest in their lives, they will eventually open up.

It's hard to believe, but even leading research suggests that kids truly want to have meaningful conversations with their parents. Dove funded a study in 2008 called *Girls, Real Pressure: A National Report on the State of Self Esteem.* When asked what they want most in their relationship with their parents, the top wish among girls was for their parents to communicate better with them, including more frequent and more open conversations, as well as discussions about what is happening in their lives.[6]

We have to believe that our kids want and need to talk with us openly. We must be persistent in opening up every opportunity for them to talk. In the car or at dinnertime, we must be prepared with questions that enable us to get into their world. There is value in simply allowing our kids to share their "high" and "low" for the day; the best and worst things they experienced. It is a non-threatening way to get them to share what's going on in their minds.

> *Jenifer's Perspective:*
> *"We have found that our kids' tongues are the most loose at bedtime. While it's tempting to ask them to come back tomorrow, we must take advantage of those moments and enter their world whenever they invite us, even if it's past our bedtime."*

3. We Must Offer Words that Show Sincere Empathy

Verse three in our story tells of Absalom's typical response to a person's grievance: *"Look, your claims are valid and proper, but there is no representative of the king to hear you."* He did for the people what Jenifer constantly has to remind me to do for her. "Show some empathy. Give me some tenderness. Validate my feelings. Tell me that I am not crazy for feeling what I am feeling." (Men, this is a "two-fer" tip, as it applies to how we connect both to our wives and our kids. Use it often!)

Nothing will draw together the hearts of two people more powerfully than offering this kind of empathetic listening. It is what powerfully bonds lifelong girlfriends (or so I am told). It is what draws the heart of a woman deeply into that of her husband. It can serve as an essential key to connecting the heart of a teenager to the heart of his or her parent. Unfortunately, parents tend to turn off their empathetic listening switch when their kids become teens. Why? Because we see much of their experiences and perspectives as shallow and immature. It is much easier to blow them off and wait for them to grow up, knowing that they will get through this time of weirdness one day.

If you take an honest look at your listening habits with your teen, this thinking might sound familiar. If it is, you shouldn't be surprised if the heart of your teenager is closed off to you. If you are aware of it, you can be certain that your son or daughter is aware of it, as well. They sense that you are not a safe place for them. In their mind, all you have to offer them are useless opinions, quick judgments, and long lectures.

We must remember that, developmentally, our kids are unable to manage stress and emotion as effectively as we are. A seemingly insignificant incident at school can produce far more anxiety in a teenager's heart and mind than a significant stressor in his parent's life. For example, while we would rate the death of a loved one a 10 on a stress scale and not being invited to a party as a 2, a teenager doesn't feel it that way. The stress and burden of not being invited feels every bit as much of a 10 as a death might. I know it sounds absurd, but it is exactly what our teenagers are experiencing inside.

When we don't acknowledge this and unintentionally "blow off" our kids' feelings by failing to offer them empathy and kind words, we are further disconnecting from their hearts. As a father, I have to discipline myself to offer understanding and emotional support to my kids when they tell me what is happening in their lives. While I want to scream "get over it; it's not a big deal," I must bite my tongue and offer gentle words of encouragement instead.

4. We Must Use Touch in an Appropriate Way

The details of Absalom's strategy offer us another key to connecting with our kids' hearts. Verse five tells us *"whenever anyone approached him to bow down before him, Absalom would reach out his hand, take hold of him and kiss him."* This no doubt provided the people with a sense that Absalom was personally concerned with being present with them in their situation. Likewise, we cannot deny the power of physical touch in connecting powerfully with our kids.

In their wonderful book *The Blessing*, Gary Smalley and John Trent remind us that one of the key elements used in the Old Testament for passing on a blessing to children is meaningful touch. This simple act, when done in an age-appropriate manner, has a unique power to communicate value and love to our children. Parents would be wise to prayerfully consider what this might look like for each of their kids.

When they were little, my kids willingly came to me for physical closeness. They would crawl into my lap or want to cuddle at bedtime. They were always open to hugs and other embraces. It was easy. As they became teenagers, things got a little more complicated.

With my teenagers, I have to creatively look for ways to give them the physical closeness that they deeply need but that they don't voluntarily seek. It means wrestling with my boys. It means gently laying my hands on my daughters' heads and saying "I love you." It means dropping *everything* in those rare moments when they do want a hug or some physical comfort. When they seek me out, I need to let them know that they are my greatest priority.

Everybody is different in regards to their need for physical touch. You must pray for insight into the needs of your particular children, as everybody needs a gentle touch at some point. Parents who want to have the hearts of their children cannot afford to ignore this.

5. We Must Bathe our Kids in Unconditional Love

While not specifically seen in the story of Absalom, we must see unconditional love as the fuel that drives the four essentials mentioned above. If we strive to connect with our kids but they suspect that our love for them is conditional, we are unlikely to have any real heart connection.

Our kids must be convinced (and we must strive to convince them) that our love for them is exactly like God's love for them: not based upon what they do or how they act, but upon who they are. Most parents are certain that they would never communicate conditional love to their kids, but it is the message that many of our teenagers are getting. They feel the heaviness of meeting our expectations and they see the joy on our faces when they do. It inadvertently assures them that they must perform to be loved.

When my kids succeed, I need to affirm them. When they fail, I need to be sure to affirm them as well. I do this by taking time to invest in them, by entering the pain of their world, by listening to them with empathy, and by touching them appropriately. All these things show them that I care. All these things communicate that I love them, no matter what. With all the pressures and challenges that our kids are facing today, they desperately need to regularly experience this type of unconditional love from their parents.

Chris Liebrum, an old youth ministry friend of mine, used to give parents an excellent litmus test of how to know whether they had their teenager's heart or not. He encouraged parents to imagine a circumstance in which their teen was out with friends on a Friday night and was being tempted to participate in some immoral or illegal activity: drinking alcohol, for example. At his moment of decision, one of two possible thoughts is going through his mind:

"If my parents find out about this, they will kill me."
Or the other possibility. . .
"If my parents find out about this, it will kill them."

Do you notice the subtle difference? The first thought shows that the kid is most worried about a possible punishment. The second thought shows that the kid is most concerned about breaking his parents' heart, most likely because the relationship has been nurtured and developed into something that the teenager values and does not want to damage.

Pursuing the hearts of our kids will be a journey that never stops. Furthermore, just as getting in shape is a lot harder than staying in shape, keeping a child's heart is much easier than trying to re-capture it once it is gone. Wise parents who want to influence their kids will focus their lives on building and nurturing a powerful love connection with them. One that evolves and changes as their kids get older. They will learn to patiently love their kids as they move through the challenges of adolescence.

Is it easy? No. Is it possible? Absolutely.

twenty-two

Mistakes

The necessity of grace when your kids (and you) fail.

The old saying goes that an ounce of prevention is worth a pound of cure. While the bulk of this book is about prevention, the fact that our families are made up of real people requires us to also talk about the cure. It would be wonderful if teaching well and setting parameters and coaching our kids toward a Godly standard for relationships and sexuality were an ironclad insurance policy against failure. But they are not. Our kids are going to fall short of God's ideal. So are we. We know this from our past and by the choices we have made since the sun came up this morning.

Some parents would disagree and insist that they are doing pretty well. This book isn't about them, after all. It's about setting their kids straight, right?

If we don't recognize the propensity towards sin in ourselves, then we probably have issues that need to be dealt with long before we deal with any issue related to our kids. For we all stand on common ground in our need for a savior. If we are looking down on our kids from an ivory tower of righteousness, then a serious perspective adjustment may be in order. I would suggest a reading of

193

Psalm 14:2-3, Romans 3:10 or Matthew 7:3. Seriously, stop reading this and examine those verses before going any further. Given our condition, we all need grace. Lots of it.

Which leads us to the issue of mistakes. Regrets. Personal failures. Whatever we choose to call it, we all have sinned and have fallen short of God's very best for us.

While there is nothing wrong with setting a high standard of purity for our kids regarding their dating relationships, we do not want to become so militant that the fear of failure leads them to hopelessness. Or even worse, that it pushes our kids to rebel. They must confidently know that their home is a place of safety and grace when they fail. And fail they will. Just as we do every day.

> *Jenifer's Perspective:*
> *"It was often hard to watch my son-in-law court*
> *and love my daughter so well, as it reminded*
> *Barrett and me of how many relational mistakes we*
> *made before we met. We experienced joy for their*
> *relationship, but plenty of regrets for us."*

As Christ described in the parable of the prodigal son, parents should always be ready to offer second chances. If our family values are more marked by right and wrong than they are by repentance and restoration, then we are missing the point. Because the primary message of the gospel is grace, not rules, there is great value in making sure that our kids clearly know that there is nothing that they can ever do that will make us stop loving them. (Tonight's homework: if your kids haven't heard that in a while, be sure to tell them before the sun goes down today.)

About a year ago, a television production company from Europe approached our church about a documentary on family life they were filming. As part of their study of ten different cultures around the world, they wanted to focus on the role that the church played in family life in the Bible Belt of America. We were thrilled to be able to participate!

Three months later, the crew arrived and we found ourselves hosting a baby shower for a young couple from our Bible study class in our small living room. Everything felt like a normal couple's shower except for the four Belgians and all their camera and sound gear.

After filming some socializing and everyone speaking blessings over the parents-to-be, the crew wanted to ask us a few questions. While they were impressed and quite moved at the outpouring of love and support from our faith community, they were interested in how we would respond if a young woman got pregnant in our church outside of marriage. Specifically, they asked me, "What if your teenage daughter told you she was pregnant?" Their post-Christian European minds were curious about how the markedly religious American would respond if things didn't go as planned.

I quickly and confidently declared that while I have taught my children Biblical values and have tried to ground them in their relationship with Christ, I know that they will mess up in both big and small ways. When they do, it is my joy to offer grace and forgiveness and to lead my kids to see how God can redeem even the most significant of mistakes. I would remind them that no sin is too big for God and that He is still in the business of taking broken people and circumstances and making them beautiful. I would lovingly lead them to experience the forgiveness of Christ and then guide them to full restoration of their relationship with God and with the people around them.

I think my atheist Belgian friends were surprised by my response because it didn't fit their framework of how they presumed our God worked. That somehow God's standard was a pass/fail test. If we don't measure up, there is punishment, consequences, and ultimately rejection. Praise God that the fundamental message of the cross is something completely different! Specifically, the cross declares some very good news for us.

We can know that we have a new status before God. *"Although you were formerly alienated and hostile in mind, engaged in evil deeds, yet He has now reconciled you in His fleshly body through death, in order to present you before Him holy and blameless and beyond reproach."* (Colossians 1:21-22) Because of the cross, the believer's identity is no longer as a sinner, but as one who stands holy and pure before God.

As has already been mentioned, we can be confident that there is *"no condemnation for those who are in Christ Jesus."* (Romans 8:1) Because of the cross, we are no longer condemned for any of our past sins.

We can be sure that God has removed our sins *"as far as the east is from the west."* (Psalm 103:12) Because of the cross, God does not deal with us on the basis of our sins, but on the fact that we know Jesus as Lord.

We must embrace this integral part of the gospel and make sure our kids know it, as well. Not only as it relates to God's mercy, but also as it relates to the grace and forgiveness we extend to them.

Practicing Grace at Home

A merciful, forgiving attitude is one thing, but what does it look like in every day life to extend grace to others? Every circumstance is different, but the tone of our response should be equal to the failure. There is no value in making a big deal out of a minor action, especially in young people who are still finding their way.

> *Jenifer's Perspective:*
> *"When my kids say something rude or a bit disrespectful to me, instead of immediately reacting, I will often say, 'Do you want a do-over?' It is my way of training our kids to realize that they have said something wrong, but that they can have a second chance to get it right without the drama of a huge correction process."*

But what about when something big happens? For example, pornography is found on the computer. A blatant lie is told about a boy/girl relationship. Somebody gets pregnant. For those times when our kids blow it in a more significant way, at the bare minimum we should train them to consider at least four key elements to restoration after a failure.

196

1. Help them to Acknowledge That They Blew It

Before seeking God's forgiveness and restoration, a person must first admit that what they have done is, in fact, sinful. A parent can try to lead his or her teenager to take ownership of their sin, but if they are convinced that they did nothing wrong then it's absolutely meaningless. Pointing a person to God's Word on the subject or issue might help, but if they don't already love and value the Scripture as the standard for their lives, there is a risk of pushing them away from God all the more. I have never met someone who enjoys getting beat over the head with the Bible.

Hopefully, key values have been outlined for them clearly so that they will know if and when they fall short of expectations. In a fundamental way, a parent can address his child's sin as a disobedience to the family's rules or ways. In this way, the command to *"obey your father and mother"* can trump just about everything. However, if the goal is also to *"not exasperate your children,"* it is a good idea to make sure that expectations are aligned with both the letter and spirit of God's Word.

If a child or teenager is going to move towards full restoration with God and others, they must first be willing to admit that they did, in fact, do something wrong and have fallen short of God's ideal. Hopefully they feel a burden of responsibility and recognize the need to make it right.

2. Lead Them to Repent and Offer Complete Forgiveness, From Both God and Us

Once a person acknowledges his or her sin, the next element of redemption is critical to the gospel message. Sadly, it is the part that we get wrong the most often. Instead of forcing our kids to make amends or to pay a price for their sin, our response should be most clearly marked by forgiveness and grace: the kind that God offers freely to all those who believe. This does not mean that punishments are not merited. There is nothing wrong with a consequence or an adjustment of privileges or rules, but those should only teach a lesson and should not affect the nature of the relationship between parent and child. Only real forgiveness can lay the groundwork for full restoration.

What the child must be guided to is the act of repentance, or turning away from their sin. Once they acknowledge that what they did was wrong, they need to turn away from it and, as Jesus told the woman caught in adultery, go and sin no more. In this decision is the promise of Christ's full forgiveness. By Biblical implication, they should also expect mom and dad's full forgiveness, as well.

Do we forget the sin? Probably not. I have personally never been able to forget something that hurt me or hurt someone I love. But forgiveness isn't forgetting. It is making the conscious decision to not deal with the person based upon the sin. One way a person can tell if forgiveness has happened is if they are still talking about it. If the transgression continues to be brought up, especially to them, then the person probably hasn't forgiven. We can help our kids to walk in Christ's forgiveness best when we model Christ's forgiveness to them when they mess up.

3. Help Them Position Themselves to Avoid the Same Mistakes in the Future

I can remember from my years as a youth minister that kids often make sincere commitments to Christ at camp or on a mission trip. I also remember that if these decisions are not followed with disciplines and a change in habits, they are likely to result in little long-term change. God can certainly stir a reaction in us at a big event, but it is when we *"work out our salvation with fear and trembling"* that God transforms our lives for the long-haul.

In the same way, many teenagers have made "abstinence pledges." Sadly, even though pledges like this are well-meaning and worth doing, statistics show that they are not particularly effective. It's not that these kids aren't well-meaning. It's just that a pledge that is made while a person continues in an unhealthy relationship probably won't stand the test of time.

Young people who have found themselves stuck in a sinful habit are often in need of a change in their environment. Walking in grace doesn't mean that we can continue to sin. Instead, it requires that we *"pay careful attention, then, to how you walk—not as unwise people but as wise."* (Ephesians 5:15) It means that we must adjust our lives in whatever way is necessary so that God can free us from the entanglements of sin.

Practically speaking, that means leading our children to remove whatever the temptation is from his or her life. It might mean leading the teenager to end a toxic relationship. Or establishing more rigid boundaries for the computer or the TV. Whatever the case, when someone is in the process of healing from the damaging affects of sin, they need loving accountability in their lives from people who love them and are committed to their wholeness. In the life of a child or teenager, nobody has more power to do this than a parent.

In addition to cleaning out some of the obvious stumbling blocks in their lives, positioning them to avoid sin will also involve a shift of focus and a renewed commitment to walking with Christ, feeding on the Scripture, and living in Christian community. Again, repentance is the first step, but grace-based and Spirit-filled discipline to re-position one's life for righteousness must come next.

There is one more thing that may need to be considered: the impact of soul-ties. One of the things that makes sexual sin so significant is that it literally binds us together with another person. In 1 Corinthians 6:16, we are asked: *"Do you not know that the one who joins himself to a harlot is one body with her? For He says, the two will become one flesh."* That intimate physical and spiritual connection is what many refer to as a "soul tie." It was not entered into lightly, so it should not be walked away from casually. Those who think they can just leave a past sexual relationship with ease are usually surprised at how much power it continues to have over them.

Great restoration and freedom can be found when a person verbally renounces the past connection and asks God to fully break the power of the relationship. Speaking it out loud can be meaningful because it is likely that the sinful covenant was made out loud in the first place. (In statements such as, "I love you. I will never leave you. I can never love anyone but you.") Freedom to move on from the past relationship might be best facilitated by renouncing the soul tie(s) in the presence of trusted and mature Christian friends, then asking

God to completely break any stronghold of power that might reside as a result of the relationship.

4. Teach Them to Live in Freedom

Just as the forgiving work of Christ on the cross is the solution to the sin of our past, it is also what we look to for hope for the future. It is the basis for which we have forgiveness, but it is also what gives us the daily right to be called *"the sons and daughters of God."* Walking in this truth is where true freedom is found.

Our deceptive and rebellious hearts lead us to believe that turning from sin and pursuing righteousness is a cumbersome pursuit. The enemy tries to convince us that walking in Christ is anything but freeing. "It's too hard," he declares. "You can never measure up to God's standard, so don't even try."

Even the most committed believers can forget that Christ came to set the captives free. Picture the powerful breakout scene from *The Shawshank Redemption*. After more than twenty years of suffering in chains, Andy Dufresne is finally free. His outstretched arms and jubilant expression tell the story of what he feels inside. In contrast to his previous bondage, he now savors the joys of freedom. Paul writes in Galatians 5:1, *"It is for freedom that Christ has set us free. Stand firm, then, and do not let yourselves be burdened again by a yoke of slavery."* With complete and unconditional forgiveness comes full and complete freedom. Satan doesn't want us to believe that.

Some days, it can be a challenge to see our new life in Christ as the source of ultimate freedom. If it's hard for adult Christ-followers to embrace this truth, then we can bet that our kids will have a hard time believing it. That's why we have to teach them that complete and lasting joy can only be found in full surrender of our lives to Jesus.

When I was a teenager, I had a lousy understanding of Christ's core message. My Christian life was motivated by fear and guilt, not freedom. This belief ultimately pushed me away from Christ, as I felt I could never bring my game up to the level of His expectations. If I couldn't measure up (and thus felt distant from Him), then I needed to work hard to get my act together before I came to Him. In some ways I felt like God was pleased with some future version of me, not

200

the person that I was in the here and now. I loved God and wanted to please Him, but I spent many years running from Him simply because I didn't understand the simple wonder and beauty of the gospel.

This is true of many of our kids as well as many of us.

My friend Tom told me the story about the time his wife attended a large women's conference with a group from their church. The group shuttled from the church to the venue in a bus each day. On the first night, the speaker passionately articulated the message of the cross. Even though Susan had been a Christian her entire adult life, the Word penetrated her heart powerfully. She experienced a fresh awe and wonder of God's complete forgiveness that is based not on what we do but on what Christ did for her at Calvary. She stayed up late that night telling Tom all that God had revealed to her.

The next morning on the bus, a woman commented that she regretted not being able to attend the night before. It broke Susan's heart to hear another woman say, "You didn't miss much. She just talked about the gospel."

May we be people who remember that the good news of our forgiveness in Christ is the essential truth of our lives. May we fully walk in that truth, knowing that His grace is sufficient for even the most shameful sins of our past. May we teach and model Christ's forgiveness to our children on those times that they fall short.

Paul assures us in 2 Corinthians 5:17 that *"If anyone is in Christ, he is a new creation; the old has passed away; behold the new has come."* (ESV) The time has come for us to start truly believing it.

If you have junk in your past or parts of your story that you regret, welcome to the club. Everybody does. However, if you claim to have a new life found in salvation through Jesus, yet these things from your past regularly fill your mind and define who you are, I want to tell you that you are doing the Christian life wrong. You are missing out on the whole point of the cross! Your old life is dead and buried. You truly are a new creation!

While this is incredibly good news for our kids when they mess up, I think it's even better news for moms and dads. While our kids are (hopefully) just getting a taste of their rebellion against God and the burden of their sins, many adults have been carrying their junk for years. Even decades. And they have not fully walked in the grace that God offers through Jesus.

It is very likely that as you read these words, something from your past is coming to mind. It is probably something you think about often—a regret or a past sin or an unhealthy relationship—but you have gotten very good at stuffing it away where nobody will notice. If you have carried it as baggage through your life, isn't it about time that you believed God's grace is sufficient even for that? You don't have to ignore what you did. You don't have to pretend it didn't happen. God knows all about it. And He loves you anyway. You can stop hiding it from Him. Instead, isn't it about time you laid it before Him in all its stinky glory and allowed Him to say, "I know you did this. I know this happened to you. But I don't care. It's not who you are. I have forgiven you completely. And I have made you into something completely different."

Wherever you are in your journey of experiencing Christ's forgiveness and restoration, allow me to remind you that it's never too late to be fully and completely forgiven. Slate wiped clean. A brand new start. That's good news, indeed.

twenty-three

Warfare

Why you must become aggressively engaged
in the fight for your kids.

When I was a teenager, I remember seeing a movie about a couple of street gangs in 1950s New York who were fighting over a disputed piece of "turf." I'm not sure if I even knew what turf was at the time. I remember being really puzzled about why a bunch of thugs would be so concerned about somebody's lawn.

Things escalated to the point of scheduling a fight in a neighborhood park where the gangs would settle things once and for all. A few days before the big night, their leaders got together to discuss the rules of the rumble. It was like a miniature Geneva Convention right there in the pool hall. I had no idea that street gangs could be so diplomatic.

In particular, I can remember them discussing what weapons could be used in the fight. One guy suggested sticks. Another said that pipes would be appropriate. One really tough guy started listing an entire arsenal of chains, knives, and guns. They debated for a while and finally decided on a few suitable "accessories" that would ensure a fair fight later that week. I thought it was a rather strange dialogue, but apparently, meetings like this happen all the time between parties in conflict.

The Silent Negotiation Between Parents & Satan

There is a war of great significance being waged over human sexuality. In our current culture and on the battlefield of the next generation, we have to admit that the church is not very effectively engaged. Moreover, as it relates to parents doing real battle in this area for the futures of our kids, we have been quite passive. If the same type of pre-fight negotiation I saw in my gang movie were to take place between Satan and most parents today, the discussion might look something like this:

Satan: *We know we can inflict maximum damage on your children with minimal effort on our part by attacking their future sexuality.*

Parents: The future is a long time from now. We aren't overly concerned.

Satan: *We will bring every resource we have to bear in this fight. We will steal their innocence early with pornographic images. We will use their peers to convince them that they need to have a boyfriend or girlfriend. We will show them through dozens of different media outlets that sexual behavior is just normal behavior. We will encourage them to fall in love and break up over and over again, making them less and less able to stay committed in a marriage relationship. We will literally bombard them with our anti-Biblical perspective until even the most committed Christ-followers see our way as totally acceptable.*

Parents: You're really going to do all that?

Satan: *Yes. That's our plan...our rules of engagement. What are you going to do about it?*

Parents: Actually, we're not going to do much of anything. Our plan is to passively let you beat the snot out of us and our kids, inflicting untold amounts of damage on the next generation, all because we are not comfortable talking about sex.

Satan: *We will see you on the battlefield.*

The likely response for all of us when considering such a negotiation is to assure ourselves that we have not been passive. After all, we have taken time to have "the talk" with our kids. We have tried hard to keep the lines of communication open. Sure, there are plenty of unengaged parents out there, but that's not us.

Before any of us assume that we have done an adequate job of equipping and protecting our children, we should consider what our kids say. According to research done by ABC's Primetime, while about 90% of parents say they've spoken to their teens about sex, only half of their teens agree.[1] There is an obvious disconnect.

Parents are not the only ones to blame for this apathy and lack of engagement. The church has remained largely silent on these issues. Pastors are reluctant to address them from the pulpit for fear that they will offend older people who deem such talk as taboo in houses of worship. Things of that nature should be dealt with privately, they reason. If only that were possible. In this day and age, these issues are as public as they have ever been.

Even youth pastors and leaders shy away from speaking the truth about the war in which our students are engaged. Many feel silenced by naïve parents who don't want their kids exposed to discussions they cannot control. Others just don't feel the urgency to deal with it because they are not aware of the long-term effects of the choices their students are making today.

So the enemy bombards our kids with lies while those tasked with giving them the truth are largely silent. It is as if we are fighting an enemy armed with rocket-propelled grenades while we are using an arsenal of squirt guns. It is obvious who is winning. The world gives a perspective over and over, and we don't say much of anything. We should not be surprised, in the absence of truth, that there is little difference between how Christian kids and their non-Christian peers approach sex and dating.

As Jennifer Parker wrote in *Christianity Today*, "Specific studies of sexual trends among Christian teens have been limited, but all indications are that, on average, there is little difference between their sexual behavior and that of non-Christian youths, other than a tendency to delay their first sexual experience slightly longer."[2] On the whole, we have done a poor job of teaching the young people of this generation what it looks like to be in the world but not of it.

Make no doubt that we have a God who wants to equip and empower us to address the relational and sexual dimensions of our children and teenagers. They are His kids, after all. When we commit ourselves to tackling these issues on behalf of our kids, we are preparing them for success on the battlefield that we know they will encounter through their teen and young adult years. More importantly, we are giving them the tools they will need to experience all the best things that God dreamed up when He first gave them life.

If we do not, they become easy targets for our enemy to pick off at his whim. We know this because human sexuality has become the spiritual battlefield that impacts more people and destroys more relationships than just about any other. Regardless of our best intentions, passivity and reluctance to talk will make us parents who continue to arm our kids with squirt guns when they are fighting an enemy who is truly armed to the teeth.

Satan's Strategy to Mess Up Our Kids

Like it or not, we are participants in an ongoing war between God and Satan for the hearts and souls of man. Without a doubt, the battlefield of human sexuality is an area of particularly violent struggle. Whether parents want to acknowledge it or not, our children are thrust into this battle at a far younger age than we can imagine. We would be wise to gain as much intelligence on our enemy as we can.

What would we see if we were able to get a glimpse into the war room of Hell? What if we could get inside the mind of our enemy and gain access to his plans and strategies? It would certainly allow us to engage in the fight with understanding. This is far better than what most do, which is blindly responding to Satan's attacks with good intentions but little direction. Thankfully, the Scriptures give us some general insight that we can apply to this particular battlefield.

First of all, we can be certain that a key component of the enemy's strategy is to destroy and distort whatever God made to be good. Jesus declares this motive in John 10:10 when He said, *"The thief comes only to steal and kill and destroy."* It stands to reason that Satan will allocate enormous resources to destroy those things that most reflect God's love and creativity. Sex surely tops the list. (In contrast, while God created fire ants, I don't imagine Satan has committed many assets to keeping them from multiplying on my lawn.) Like nothing else in God's creation, sex is a beautiful act that reflects our Creator's heart, and it is the most powerful and tangible way that two people can connect in love and intimacy. Satan hates that.

Similarly, if one of Satan's goals is to derail the work of Christ in this world, he can do this best by derailing God's people. We can be sure that he will strike aggressively at the primary human institution that God gives us as a picture of our relationship with Him: the marriage between a man and a woman. We can see Christian marriages falling apart at almost the same rate as the rest of the world. Clearly, his strategy to destroy marriage doesn't begin when a couple walks down the aisle. It starts far sooner. If Satan can encourage young people to develop habits and collect emotional baggage that they can carry into their marriages, he can cause all sorts of pain that will fully reveal itself later.

A third thing we can be sure of is that a large portion of Satan's budget is devoted to marketing. Much like an effective advertiser, he convinces us that we desperately need whatever he is selling. Unfortunately, Satan's marketing is based entirely upon lies. Again, Jesus calls Satan out in John 8:44 when he describes him as *"a murderer from the beginning, not holding to the truth, for there is no truth in him. When he lies, he speaks his native language, for he is a liar and the father of lies."* He takes the very thing that has the potential to destroy us and dresses it up in such a way that we become convinced that we cannot live without it. Again, this is clearly his strategy when it comes to us experiencing our sexuality outside of God's parameters.

Finally, we can know that Satan will show no mercy when it comes to the weak and the innocent. Consider 1 Peter 3:8. *"Be alert and of sober mind. Your enemy the devil prowls around like a roaring lion looking for someone to devour."* A television show about African wildlife on a nature channel gives us an excellent mental picture of this. A predator will always pick out the most weak and frail animal from within a herd to single out for his lunch. The Scripture uses this very word picture to describe the strategies of our enemy. While most of humanity shows leniency on the young, we must remember that Satan shows no such compassion. He will not hesitate to set his sights on our kids.

If I Were Satan, This is What I Would Do

I may not have the ability to sneak into the war room of Hell for a peek at what our enemy is up to, but, based on what I know of him from Scripture, I can presume what I would do if I were him. With that in mind, allow me to put a new spin on the role of "Devil's Advocate." Specifically, let me outline a suggested plan of what I would do on the "sexual battlefield" if I were Satan.

If I were Satan, I would task my "best people" with messing up human sexuality. This would not be a passive attack, but a full-frontal assault with all the powers of darkness at my disposal. A key part of this would be a deceptive plan to convince people that their sexuality was a simple biological drive, not a critical dimension of their spiritual lives.

I would lull parents into a deep passivity, keeping them distracted from the needs of their kids. I would make them busy with work, sports, church, and the simple management of home in such a way that they are oblivious to their lack of meaningful relationships with their children.

If I were Satan, I would give special attention to destroying the father/daughter relationship. If I can shift a girl's unsatisfied longing for her father's heart over to the desire for a boyfriend and the attention he offers her, there's nothing I can't do to mess up her life. That girl becomes one that I can literally destroy with both hands tied behind my back.

I would lead families to believe that sex is a taboo subject. I would make it awkward and uncomfortable for parents and kids to discuss. That way, when a young person had a question about their feelings or their experience, the last place they would dream of going for answers would be their parents.

Some of the greatest tools of deception are false assumptions. Therefore, I would lead church leaders to assume that parents are teaching their kids about these issues. Likewise, I would lead parents to assume that the church is doing it. That would leave kids exactly where I want them: alone and defenseless.

I would convince moms that it is the dad's job to guard the hearts and minds of their children. I would convince dads that it is a mom's job. Furthermore, I would create as much conflict between husbands and wives on this issue as possible, leading to frustration and paralysis.

I would use whatever means necessary to encourage kids to grow up quickly and lose their innocence. I would infiltrate their TV shows with boyfriend/girlfriend plot lines to convince girls that they desperately need a boy to like them. I would expose them to sexual images early on so that boys learn early that women are objects to be used.

I would put tons of energy into convincing young people that, in the area of sex, the world is credible and their parents are clueless. I would take every opportunity to confirm for them that casual sex is fun and exciting, and that sex within marriage is dull and boring. Movies, TV, and music would be the ideal mediums for this message.

I would saturate the world with sexual images, making sure that young people, in general, and boys in particular, get exposed to them at an early age. I would take the lessons gleaned from my associates working in the cigarette industry: if we can get them hooked early, we will have a customer for life.

I would do all I can to mess up the sex lives of married couples, making them feel inadequate or incapable of teaching their kids on the subject. If I could make it a distasteful subject for parents, then talking about it with their kids will be distasteful, as well.

Finally, I would trick parents into thinking that they have plenty of time to teach their children about sex, dating, and the power of emotional relationships. I would work to make sure that their children encounter these issues long before mom and dad ever bring them up.

This is what I would do if I were Satan. But what I would do does not matter. What matters is what he is actually doing. Crafty as he is, Satan typically stays a step or two ahead of most believers, so my list is surely incomplete. He is likely doing all that I suggested and much more. If that is the case, then a strategic and aggressive response is needed. It is time for parents to act.

twenty-four

Lifeguards

*It's time to start diligently looking out for the kids
that God has called us to protect.*

When my kids were young, we lived in a town with a great community pool. It was one of the early-adopters of the miniature water park model that has become so popular these days. It had a few water slides, a "splash pad" with spraying water shooting in every direction and a zero-entry pool that felt like a beach. My kids loved it and so did I.

Though it was one of our favorite places to go in the summer, there was one thing about the pool that always annoyed our kids: the lifeguards. They were the most somber and focused team of lifeguards ever assembled. They didn't smile. They didn't talk. To make things even worse, their rules were over-the-top. For example, while it's not uncommon to have a "no diving" rule in the shallow end of some pools, this place had a "no jumping" rule. Kids literally couldn't get into the pool by jumping feet first. They had to "ease" in. After five years of living there, I still got yelled at for breaking that rule.

I remember the training exercises that the staff would do about every half hour. They would throw a big pink playground ball into the water, simulating a child in trouble. The closest lifeguard would blow an air horn and jump into the pool (I guess the rules didn't apply to them) for a "rescue." Every other lifeguard would point at the incident while another reserve lifeguard would quickly step into the place of the rescuer. It was a well-orchestrated dance and it was always amazing to watch.

As much as we hated all the strict rules and regulations at that pool, one thing is true: as parents, we never worried about our kids' safety while we were there. We knew that the staff had a serious perspective on watching out for the well-being of the swimmers.

Contrast that lifeguard experience with another one I had about a year ago.

Jenifer's family had come to Amarillo, Texas from across the country (and from around the world) for her grandmother's funeral. As is often true when an older saint dies, her funeral was both a time to celebrate a well-lived life and a good excuse for a family reunion. We all stayed at a nice new hotel that had a small indoor pool with a water slide. Needless to say, all our young kids thought that this was awesome.

When we checked in, we were told that the pool was open but that they only operated the waterslide when their lifeguard was present. Our kids anxiously waited for that evening when her shift started.

For the purposes of this story, know that I use the term "lifeguard" very loosely. In actuality, I would not have trusted the girl who was tasked with "guarding our lives" to pet-sit a hamster. When we arrived that night to swim, the slide was open and dozens of kids were crammed into the tiny pool, but I didn't notice a lifeguard… until I looked over in the corner of the pool area. There, sitting on a cabinet full of towels, head leaned back on the wall, earbuds from an iPod in her ears, bored expression on her face, was a 15-year-old girl. She was our lifeguard.

The girl was uninterested at best, completely distracted at worst. As my 4-year-old daughter played in the pool with her cousins, I had zero confidence that the lifeguard on duty could be trusted to watch out for her. In fact, her presence was so entirely benign that the word "useless" came to mind. Here was a person tasked with the responsibility of keeping children safe who obviously had no interest in the job and who did not recognize the urgency of the task. While my kids certainly enjoyed the freedom of sliding and playing with no rules or restrictions, I witnessed numerous incidents when kids were taking risks and putting themselves in danger. And the lifeguard said nothing. The lifeguard did nothing. In effect, the lifeguard was good for nothing.

Parents = Lifeguards

With regards to protecting our kids from the relational and sexual dynamics of our culture, we have a choice. We can be vigilant and deliberate like the lifeguards at my community water park, or we can neglect our responsibilities like the girl at the hotel pool. To be completely honest, my experience shows that most parents are more like the latter: generally ineffective.

These parents may be excellent in most every way, providing every opportunity for their kids to be successful. They monitor their kids' schoolwork and expect good effort and grades from their kids. They provide their kids with specialized coaching in sports, music, and other extracurricular activities. They strive to teach their kids a moral (even Biblical) worldview, getting them to church and helping them to be good and honest and kind.

In just about every way, the contemporary American parent demonstrates love and care and leadership to their kids. But many of these lifeguards have a glaring deficiency in one significant area. When it comes to helping their kids to figure out relationships and navigate their sexuality and maintain their purity, the kids are left to fend for themselves.

Another group of parents are more like the diligent lifeguards at my old neighborhood pool. These parents don't have everything figured out. They might even have some brokenness in their own pasts. Still, they are aware of how high the stakes are, and they know that their kids need them to watch out for them. Most importantly, they are looking to God for insight and courage to know what to do.

While Joshua 1:9 was a specific word given by God to a leader before His people took the Promised Land, parents facing these issues need the general encouragement that God offers us through this passage. God said, *"Have I not commanded you? Be strong and courageous. Do not be terrified; do not be discouraged, for the Lord your God will be with you wherever you go."* If any task is terrifying and requires ongoing encouragement from God, it is this one. Courageous parents who want to prepare their kids for a healthy marriage and sexuality desperately need God's help. The great thing is that He is with us. He will come alongside any parent who takes these issues seriously and delves into them headfirst with their kids.

The time has come for us to take a good, long look in the mirror. We must ask God to reveal to us what type of parents we are. Which of the lifeguards do we most resemble? If we have been aware of this responsibility, we must daily ask God to help us. If we have neglected it or carelessly approached it, we must commit ourselves to the task. We must see this as a critical dimension of raising our kids.

Finally, if we feel the heaviness of these issues but have been paralyzed due to our own failures, then we need to allow God to get to work in our lives in some fresh, new ways. We have a God who restores. He is a God who takes broken people and makes them whole again. He is the only One who can enable us to do what we cannot do on our own.

None of that can come from our own strength. It must come from our dependence upon God and a constant yielding to the leadership of the Holy Spirit. When we parent our kids in our own power, rarely do we have any understanding of what is really going on, and seldom do we know what to do about it. This is particularly true when it comes to the internal matters of the typical child's heart. Their emotions are confusing and powerful forces that need our constant care and attention. We desperately need God's help!

It's Time to Act

In reading these words you may become aware of the issues and become immediately and overwhelmingly concerned. This might lead to a desire to lock your kids away until they are 25. Or it might lead to utter helplessness due to the fact that it seems you are fighting an uphill battle. Hopefully, though, it will serve as a catalyst that stirs you to do something.

Becoming informed and equipped parents who are comparable to the right kind of lifeguards will not happen automatically just because you care. It will require you to take action on at least a few things. Here are some places to start.

1. Get Both Parents on Essentially the Same Page

For married and divorced parents alike, these are issues that must be considered by both mom and dad. One parent trying to lead and guide and protect his or her kids will struggle if the other parent does not share the same convictions. If the parents are struggling then we can be sure that the kids will struggle, being unsure of what the values and rules are. The most practical solution to address this is for both parents to be exposed to the same principles and paradigms, if only to serve as a starting place for discussion. If you are reading this book alone, it would be highly recommended that you suggest that your spouse read it, as well. Unless both of you have a sense of conviction about these issues, there will be no clear direction for what your family should do.

2. Evaluate Where Your Kids Are

Prayerfully take a good look at each of your kids—their ages, development, environment, etc.—to determine what issues and topics might need to be addressed. You should pray that God would grant you insight to recognize the unique challenges that your kids might be struggling with that you might have overlooked. There might be a temptation to put things off and to wait a little longer. For the last time, know that the vast majority of parents arrive way too late. Wise parents will take an honest evaluation and prayerfully consider how to get there sooner.

3. Develop a Plan

In addition to giving some directed attention to any current issues of developmental relevance, you would be wise to begin laying out a plan for the future. This might involve discussions of a philosophical nature. For example, "What is our family's view of dating?" "What parameters will we set in the future?" Beyond establishing some general guidelines, your family should develop some sort of plan to train and equip your kids for Biblical thinking on the issue of relationships, particularly opposite-sex ones. It will look different for every family, but Christ-focused relational principles should be addressed just as issues of character and spiritual development are.

4. Take a Few Small Steps as Soon as Possible

The ever-zealous (and very effective) lifeguards at my neighborhood pool were constantly training and always taking steps to stay sharp in carrying out their responsibilities. In contrast, a lifeguard who carelessly stares at a body of water will become accustomed to doing nothing. When a crisis comes, he or she will likely be caught off guard. As with any important thing that parents endeavor to do, good intentions can easily turn into passive neglect. The solution for parents who want to take action is to simply do that: take action. Identify a dimension of your particular child's developing sexual awareness. Pray for insight on how to address it and look for an opportunity to connect meaningfully with the heart of your child in a teachable moment. Then act. This doesn't need to be something huge but it needs to be something deliberate.

5. Surround Yourself with Other Like-Minded Parents

Let us openly identify the proverbial elephant in the room. Most of what has been shared in the pages of this book is pretty counter-cultural. Hopefully, the truths will resonate with many. But we cannot deny that the overwhelming momentum of our sexually-charged culture is moving in one direction, and it is not for the better. Parents who commit to being intentional in guiding and guarding their kids in these areas will likely feel very alone. To stay encouraged and to maintain a measure of sanity, parents will need other, like-minded families to walk through life with: people who are raising their kids with similar values and will remind them that they are not crazy. This is especially needed during the teen years when parents are often isolated. Jenifer and I have often felt alone in our convictions, but our closest friends always remind us that God is at work and that we should continue to be counter-cultural. Nothing is more encouraging.

I take that back. One thing is more encouraging: a clear calling by God. If God is calling you to do something, then you can be confident that He will be with you as you do it.

His promise to His disciples in Matthew 28:20 could not be any clearer: *"I am with you always."* The fancy Greek translation of the word "always" in that passage of Scripture is simply that: "always." (His promise is not complicated.) If God calls us to follow Him, then He will not bail on us when we take risky steps of obedience. Oftentimes, nothing feels more risky than talking to our kids about their sexuality. But we should not fear. He is always with those who know Him as Lord.

If God is calling you to coach and disciple your kids to see that their sexuality is a gift created by and given to them by God, then He will be with you. You will know the peace that comes from reclaiming His Truth in the midst of so many distortions.

If God is calling you to stand in the gap for the sake of your kids, offering protection and guidance through some of their most tumultuous days, then He will be with you. You will know the confidence that is found when you stand for the things for which God stands.

If God is calling you to aggressively take back ground that the enemy has stolen from humanity regarding our enjoyment of fulfilling sexuality, then He will be with you. You will be able to savor the joy that comes from knowing your spouse in a deep and intimate way such that only a creative and wise God could have dreamed up.

You must know that God has called you, that God is for you, and that God is with you. As you live your life dependent upon Him, He promises to help you. He is cheering you on. In spite of the brokenness of our world and the overwhelming challenge of swimming upstream in a current that is so very strong, He is there. He is near to each one of us, surrounding us with His presence and

His power. If we will only petition Him for wisdom and guidance and help, He will give it to us freely.

Right now would be a great time to ask Him.

And tomorrow.

And so would the day after that.

In fact, perhaps the most wise and God-honoring thing you could possibly do with your life is to daily seek His still, small voice of love and leadership and comfort. He's crazy about you. He's crazy about your kids. Don't believe me? Just ask Him. Check it out in His Word. It's true. God is calling each of us to lead our kids to an abundantly full life, which just so happens to (eventually) include an abundantly full sex life. But our kids need us to help them to not mess it up.

So let's get started...

End Notes

Chapter 1: Time Travel

1. National Center for HIV/Aids, Viral Hepatitis, STD, and TB Prevention: Division of Adolescent and School Health. (2011). *Trends in the prevalence of sexual behaviors and HIV testing: National YRBS: 1991-2011* [Data file]. Retrieved from http://www.cdc.gov/Healthy Youth/yrbs/pdf.us_sexual_trends_yrbs.pdf
2. Stepp, L. S. (2005, September 16). Study: Half of all teens have had oral sex. *The Washington Post.* Retrieved from http://www.seniorreligion.com/new_page_363.htm
3. Forhan, S. E., Gottlieb, S. L., Sternberg, M. R., Xu, F., Datta, S. D., McQuillan, G. M., et al. (2009). Prevalence of sexually transmitted infections among female adolescents aged 14 to 19 in the United States. *Pediatrics*, *124*(6), 1505-1512.
4. The National Campaign to Prevent Teen and Unplanned Pregnancy. (2002). *Teens' attitudes toward marriage, cohabitation, and divorce.* Retrieved from http://www.thenationalcampaign.org/resources /pdf/SS/SS16_Marriage.pdf
5. English, Bella. The Secret Life of Boys: Pornography is a Mouse Click Away, and Kids Are Being Exposed to it in Ever-increasing Numbers. *The Boston Globe*, May 12, 2005.
6. Holmes, David. (2013, November 19). *Infographic: Is internet porn destroying our sex lives?* Retrieved from http://pando.com/2013/11/19/infographic-is-internet-porn-destroying-our-sex-lives/
7. Barna Research Group. *Americans are most likely to base truth on feelings.* Press release. February 12, 2002.

Chapter 2: High Stakes

1. The National Campaign to Prevent Teen and Unplanned Pregnancy. (2009, December). *Special tabulations of the national survey of reproductive and contraceptive knowledge.* Retrieved from http://www.npr.org/internedition/fall11/wp-content/uploads/2011/12/NAmun_Evangelical-Young-Adults-Confused-About-Sex.pdf
2. Ibid.
3. Smyth, P. J. (2011, August) *Getting ready for marriage.* E-book. Page 27. Retrieved from http://truthresources.co.za/wp-content/uploads/2011/08/Relationships_And_Sexuality.pdf
4. Paik, A. (2011). Adolescent sexuality and risk of marital dissolution. *Journal of Marriage and Family*, 73, 472-485.

5. Teachman, J. (2003). Premarital sex, premarital cohabitation, and the risk of subsequent marital dissolution among women. *Journal of Marriage and Family,* 65, 444-455.
6. Rector, R. E., et al. (2003). *The harmful effects of early sexual activity and multiple sexual partners among women: a book of charts.* The Heritage Foundation. 2003. Retrieved from http://s3.amazonaws.com/thf_media/2003/pdf/Bookofcharts.pdf
7. Regnerus, M. (2007). *Forbidden fruit: Sex and religion in the lives of american teenagers.* Add location: Oxford University Press

Chapter 3: The Playground

1. Ryan, K. *Finding Your Prince in a Sea of Toads.* Wnumclaw, WA: Winepress, 2011.
2. Boteach, S. (2010, October). *How the condom culture is killing sex.* Retrieved from http://www.huffingtonpost.com/rabbi-shmuley-boteach/how-the-condom-culture-is_b_758432.html.

Chapter 4: Foolishness

1. Paulsen, H A. *Emotional Purity: An Affair of the Heart.* Enumclaw, WA: Winepress, 2001. Page 30.
2. Paulsen, H. A. (2007, June 9). *The emotional purity blog.* Retrieved from http://emotionalpurity.blogspot.com/2007/06/emotional-puirty.html
3. You can see the video of "Who's Gonna Save My Soul?" at www.youtube.com/watch?v=W4bvRamMiY4. Be warned: it's pretty gory.

Chapter 6: The Opposite-sex

1. http://www.merriam-webster.com/dictionary/schema
2. http://dictionary.reference.com/browse/schema?s=t
3. The Blimeycow Channel. (2012, April 9). *Messy Mondays: "Seven Tips for Successful Dating."* Retrieved from https://www.youtube.com/watch?v=lqkMAiShiSY
4. Miller, B.& Olsen, T. As cited in Jeannie Echenique, "Early Dating May Lead to Early Sex." USA Today, 12 November 1986, D1.

Chapter 7: Birds and Bees

1. Ten Boom, C. *The Hiding Place.* Peabody, MA: Hendrickson, 2009. Page 30.

Chapter 9: Modesty

1. Barry, D. *Dave Barry's Complete Guide to Guys: A Fairly Short Book.* New York: Fawcett Columbine, 1996. Page 108.

Chapter 11: Selfishness

1. Jay, M. (2012, April 14). The downside of cohabitating before marriage. *The New York Times Sunday Review.* Retrieved from http://www.nytimes.com/2012/04/15/opinion/sunday/the-downside-of-cohabiting-before-marriage.html?pagewanted=all&_r=0
2. Popenoe, D. & Whitehead, B. D.. (2013, January). *Should we live together: What young adults need to know about cohabitation before marriage.* The National Marriage Project. Retrieved from http://nationalmarriageproject.org/wp-content/uploads/2013/01/ShouldWeLiveTogether.pdf

Chapter 12: Reality

1. Driscoll, M. (2008, February 22). *"Too Young To Date?"* Retrieved from https://www.youtube.com/watch?v=UnEF9_R1ctI

Chapter 13: Chemistry

2. McIlhaney, J. S., & Bush, F. M. *Hooked: New science on how casual sex is affecting our children.* Chicago: Northfield, 2008.
3. Charles, T. (2011, September). Almost everyone's doing it. *Relevant Magazine.* Retrieved from http://www.relevantmagazine.com/life/relationships/almost-everyones-doing-it
4. Hamilton, L. A. et al. (2012) *Sex Talk,* a University of Arizona Campus Health Service Publication. Retrieved from http://www.health.arizona.edu/health_topics/sexual_health/sextalk/2012/sextalk%2010.22.12%20online.pdf
5. Gungor, M. Paraphrased from the *Laugh Your Way to a Better Marriage* video, Part 4: "The Number One Key to Incredible Sex"(the first 8 minutes of the introduction). Available from www.laughyourway.com.
6. Teachman, J. (2003). Premarital sex, premarital cohabitation, and the risk of subsequent marital dissolution among women. *Journal of Marriage and Family,* 65, 444-455.
7. The Social Pathologist Blog. (2012, March 27). Retrieved from http://socialpathology.blogspot.com/2012/03/promiscuity-data-guest-post.html
8. McIlhaney, J. S., & Bush, F. M. Page 51.

Chapter 14: Unity

1. Jay, M. (2012, April 15). *The downside of cohabiting before marriage.* Retrieved from http://www.nytimes.com/2012/04/15/opinion/sunday/ the-downside-of-cohabiting-before-marriage.html?pagewanted=all&_r=0

Chapter 16: Technology

1. Matlock, M. *Raising Wise Children.* Grand Rapids, MI: Zondervan, 2012.

Chapter 17: Pornography

1. XXX.church.com, 2012
2. Ferree, Marnie (2010). *No stones: women redeemed from sexual addiction.* Downers Grove, Illinois: Intervarsity Press.
3. Dobson, J. C. (2000). *Preparing for adolescence.* Ventura, Calif: Gospel Light.
4. Wolf, Naomi. The porn myth. *The New York Times Online.* Retrieved from http://nymag.com/nymetro/news/trends/n_9437/
5. Dr. Chap Clark, as quoted at a live presentation on understanding teenagers held in Marietta, Georgia on January 29, 2010.
6. Feldhahn, S. C. (2004). *For women only: What you need to know about the inner lives of men.* Sisters, OR: Multnomah Publishers.
7. Robinson, M. (2010, January 11). Cupid's poisoned arrow. *Psychology Today Online.* Retrieved from http://www.psychologytoday.com/blog/cupids-poisoned-arrow/201001/was-the-cowardly-lion-just-masturbating-too-much
8. *A generation of perverts, pimps and whores: How internet porn has removed love from the sex lives of today's teens.* Retrieved from http://patdollard.com/2010/01/a-generation-of-perverts-pimps-and-whores-how-internet-porn-has-removed-love-from-the-sex-lives-of-todays-teens/
9. Arterburn, S., Stoeker, F., & Yorkey, M. (2000). *Every man's battle: Winning the war on sexual temptation.* Colorado Springs, CO: WaterBrook Press.

Chapter 19: Marriage

1. Lapp, D. (2011, February 11). Did I get married too young? *The Wall Street Journal.* Retrieved from http://online.wsj.com/article/SB10001424052748704107204575039150739864666.html
2. Regnerus, M. (August 2009). The case for early marriage. *Christianity Today.*
3. Lapp.
4. Regnerus.
5. Ibid.

Chapter 20: Abuse

1. Saul, J. and Audage, N. (2007). United States Department of Health & Human Services. Centers for Disease Control and Prevention. *Preventing Child Sexual Abuse Within Youth Serving Organizations: Getting Started on Policies and Procedures.* Atlanta: National Center for Injury Prevention Control.

2. List compiled by The Child Molestation Research and Prevention Institute. Copyright 2007.

Chapter 21: Influence

1. Hunter, B., & Blair, K. *From Santa to sexting: Helping your child safely navigate middle school and shape the choices that last a lifetime.* Abilene, TX: Leafwood Publishers.
2. GFK Roper Youth Report. (2012). *Influences on youth decisions about drinking.* Retrieved from http://www.alcoholstats.com/uploads/InfluencesOnYouthsDecisionsAboutDrinking.pdf.
3. The National Campaign to Prevent Teen and Unplanned Pregnancy. (2012). *With one voice 2012: Highlights from a survey of teens and adults about teen pregnancy and related issues.* Retrieved from http://www.thenationalcampaign.org/resources/pdf/briefly-wov-2012-highlights.pdf
4. Ibid.
5. Coley, R. L., Votruba-Drzal, E., & Schindler, H. S. (2009). Fathers' and mothers' parenting predicting and responding to adolescent sexual risk behaviors. *Child Development*, 80: 808–827.
6. Dove Self-Esteem Fund Study. (2008, October 8). *Girls, real pressure: A national report on the state of self esteem.* Retrieved from http://www.aauw-nys.org/attached%20files/district/District%207%20Bullying%20Conference%20Materials%20Spring%202012/Value%20U/Media%20Literacy/SelfEsteem_Report.pdf

Chapter 23: Warfare

1. *What parents don't know about their teen daughters' sex lives.* Primetime. May 18, 2006. Can be viewed online at http://abcnews.go.com/Primetime/Health/story?id=1974232&page=1#.UW830YLq5ec
2. Parker, J. (March, 2003).The sex lives of Christians. *Christianity Today.*

Recommended Books and Resources

The Blessing by Gary Smalley and John Trent

The Chicken's Guide to Talking Turkey with your Kids About Sex by Kevin Leman

Emotional Purity by Heather Paulson

Every Young Man's Battle by Steven Arterburn

For Young Women Only by Shaunti Feldhahn

Forbidden Fruit: Sex and Religion in the Lives of American Teenager by Mark Regnerus

From Santa to Sexting by Brenda Hunter

God's Design for Sex published by NavPress

Hooked: New Science on How Casual Sex is Affecting our Children by Joe McIlhaney, Jr. and Freda McKissic Bush

Interviewing Your Daughter's Date by Dennis Rainey

Learning About Sex for the Christian Family (Boys and Girls Editions) by Concordia

Passport to Purity audio series published by FamilyLife

Point Man by Steve Farrar

Preparing Your Son for Every Young Man's Battle by Steven Arterburn

The Princess and the Kiss by Jennie Bishop

Raising a Modern Day Knight by Robert Lewis

Search for Significance by Robert McGee

What are You Waiting For? by Dannah Gresh

What He Must Be to Marry My Daughter by Voddie Baucham

Your Girl by Vicki Courtney

About the Author

Barrett Johnson is the husband to Jenifer, the father of five great kids (including four adolescents), and the youngest and coolest grandfather you have ever met. He has served as the Family Minister at Johnson Ferry Baptist Church outside of Atlanta for 8 years. Before that, his 15 years of youth ministry experience helped fuel his unique perspective on these issues. Barrett has degrees from Texas A&M University and Southwestern Seminary, but has received his best education through the no-holds-barred nature of everyday family life. Barrett and Jenifer love coaching regular families to experience God's very best in their homes.

About INFO for Families

I.N.F.O.

"INFO" is an acronym for "Imperfect & Normal Families Only." The premise is that there is no such thing as a perfect family. All of us struggle in some way; but we have an extraordinary God who wants to lead us to success. The ministry of Barrett and Jenifer Johnson has always been marked by raw honesty, faithfulness to Scripture, and a commitment to tackling head-on the challenges that families face. After all, they are part of an imperfect and normal family, too.

The name INFO for Families was first coined five years ago as the name of their blog. It was created to supplement Barrett's pastoral ministry that was focused on coaching families to live Biblically, grow spiritually, and connect in meaningful ways in their most important relationships. The blog currently has more than 40,000 monthly page views.

Go to www.infoforfamilies.com to find out more.
Like us... facebook.com/INFOforFamilies
Follow us... twitter.com/INFOforFamilies
Get all crafty... pinterest.com/INFOforFamilies

INFO FOR
FAMILIES
resources

Coming in 2014:

Age-Focused "Companions" to *The Talk(s)*

These short, downloadable e-books describe specific developmental milestones, suggest key challenges for which parents need to prepare their kids, and offer practical ideas for talking about these issues. Five different volumes for five unique stages that every family will pass through:

- **Children from 5-9**

- **Preteens from 10-12**

- **Middle Schoolers from 13-14**

- **High Schoolers from 15-18**

- **Young Adults from 19 and Up**

These helpful guides will give specific direction to what you can be doing NOW to prepare your kids to both think right and choose right.

Go to www.infoforfamilies.com to find out more.

If you feel the content of *The Talk(s)* would be appropriate to share in your church, school, or community setting, consider hosting a live event. Barrett and Jenifer can speak in a number of formats on a variety of topics related to Biblical sexuality as it connects with family life.

For Parents. . .

"RAISING PURE KIDS – A Parent's Guide to Talking about Sex, Dating, and other Unmentionables."

This workshop covers many of the issues addressed in *The Talk(s)* and covers both "what to know" and "what to do." It is great for parents of teenagers but ideal for parents of older elementary aged-children. The conference can be shared in a variety of formats, from a 4-hour conference that includes a Q and A to a shorter 90-minute event that covers the key issues. Barrett also has a 45-minute presentation that can serve as an effective plenary message.

For Families with Teenagers. . .

"MAKING WISE CHOICES – Honest Conversations about Sex, Dating, and Other Unmentionables."

This event is perfect for churches and groups looking to offer this content to teenagers and parents together. Barrett and Jenifer lead an innovative workshop that launches families into important discussions about the implications of our sexualized culture, the need to operate differently from the world, and the Biblical design for healthy sexuality. This event can be done in a variety of time formats.

232

For Women. . .

"The Married Girl's Guide to Great Sex" (Jen only)

Many of God's girls have a view of sex that has been tarnished and distorted by our world. This one-day conference is designed to help women discover why God created sex and to give them a Biblical perspective of how intimacy can bring strength and joy to their marriages. It provides a safe place where married women can recapture a healthy picture of something God made to be incredible and beautiful.

Other Marriage and Parenting Events

Barrett and Jenifer teach together on a variety of topics, including:

- Marriage Prep (for engaged couples)
- Recapturing Intimacy (God's design for passion and sex)
- Marriage Tune-Up (for couples of all ages)
- Surviving Marriage at Mid-Life (ideal for couples married for 15-30 years)
- Becoming a Fearless Family (How to face your fears and trust in God)
- Effective Parenting in the Home (practical & Biblical principles for parenting)
- How to Make Disciples as You Raise Your Kids (discipleship in the home)

For more information, you can contact Barrett and Jenifer via email at infoforfamilies@gmail.com or on the web at www.infoforfamilies.com.

Made in the USA
San Bernardino, CA
28 April 2014